A Great & Godly Adventure

A
Great & Godly
Adventure

The Pilgrims &
the Myth of
the First Thanksgiving

GODFREY HODGSON

PublicAffairs
New York

Published in the United States by PublicAffairs™,
a member of the Perseus Books Group.

Book design by Jane Raese
Text set in 12-point Adobe Caslon

Library-of-Congress Cataloging-in-Publication Data
Hodgson, Godfrey.
A great and godly adventure : the Pilgrims and the myth of the first Thanksgiving /
Godfrey Hodgson.—1st ed.
cm.
Includes index.
ISBN-13: 978-1-58648-373-9
ISBN-10: 1-58648-373-0
1. Pilgrims (New Plymouth Colony) 2. Thanksgiving Day—History.
3. Massachusetts—History—New Plymouth, 1620–1691.
4. Wampanoag Indians—History—17th century. 5. Indians of North America—
First contact with Europeans—Massachusetts. I. Title.
F68.H69 2006
974.4'02—dc22
2006049373

ISBN-13: 978-1-58648-373-9
ISBN-10: 1-58648-373-0

FIRST EDITION

1 3 5 7 9 10 8 6 4 2

Contents

Prologue:
Thanksgiving

They are the gracious gifts of the Most High God . . . .
I do therefore invite my fellow citizens in every part of
the United States . . . to set apart and observe the last Thursday
of November next, as a day of Thanksgiving and Praise to
our beneficent Father who dwelleth in the Heavens.
—ABRAHAM LINCOLN

Twas founded be th' Puritans to give thanks f'r bein' presarved
fr'm th'Indyans, an' . . . we keep it to give thanks
we are presarved from the Puritans.
—FINLEY PETER DUNNE

EVERY NOVEMBER TENS OF MILLIONS OF AMERICANS
travel great distances in order to gather together with the
family to celebrate the warmest and best-beloved of the national
holidays: Thanksgiving. In 2005, some 37 million Americans traveled more than fifty miles to be with the folks, in spite of gas at

around \$2.45 a gallon, heavy traffic, and dangerous roads. (In 2004, 560 people were killed in traffic accidents, more than 40 percent of them alcohol related.) More than four million flew home for the holiday, undeterred by high fares, ticket lines, and two-hour delays to go through screening. Many tens of millions more, who do not have to travel great distances to be with their families, celebrate the holiday at home.

Independence Day is an occasion for drums and bugles, fireworks and public oratory. Thanksgiving, in contrast, is a private feast: a quiet meal of turkey and cranberry sauce, and many other good things, including pumpkin pie, taken in the intimacy of a family home. It is a festival that comes even closer than the Fourth of July to the deepest of all American national feelings: gratitude for God's special providence for the United States as a nation of immigrants who have lived for the most part in peace and plenty under the rule of law as established with the consent of the governed.

Inclusiveness, too, is always a vital part of the spirit of Thanksgiving, and that has often meant including in the family feast those who have not been so fortunate and those who have no other table to sit down at on the holiday. At what is remembered as the First Thanksgiving, Pilgrims and Indians feasted together. Not long after that, Indians were generally not at the party. Recently they have been included again. For many New Americans, Thanksgiving has been especially important because it expresses a willingness in the host society to welcome immigrants to the national plenty.

Quiet and unpretentious as it is, Thanksgiving also expresses deep religious impulses. Christians recognize in it an echo of the breaking of bread that is at the heart of their observance, while Jews have often seen it as a kind of seder, in that it commemorates, by a shared meal, a journey toward salvation. Its most fundamental meaning, though, is gratitude. In that respect it is one representation of a religious instinct that is both primal and virtually universal. In almost every culture, men and women have gathered when the crops were in to thank the God or gods of nature for their food, and to pray that it would continue for another year.

The celebration of Thanksgiving recalls, across almost four centuries, something of the emotions felt by the first successful European settlers as they looked back on what they had achieved, and what their God had vouchsafed them since they began life in an unfamiliar continent so full of danger and promise. It seemed proper to remember the nation's forefathers, and what came to be called Thanksgiving was often called Forefathers' Day. Years after he led his companions ashore, to express those feelings William Bradford reached instinctively for the sonorous language of the Old Testament.

> May not and ought not the children of these fathers rightly say: Our fathers were Englishmen which came over this great ocean, and were ready to perish in this wilderness, but they cried unto the Lord, and He heard their voice and looked on their adversity . . . . Let them therefore praise the Lord, because he is good: and his mercies endure forever. Yea let them which have been redeemed of the Lord show how He hath delivered them from the hand of the oppressor. . . . Let them confess before the Lord His loving kindness and His wonderful works before the sons of men.[1]

Two images capture something of what Thanksgiving has meant over nearly four centuries. The first is an eyewitness description, by one of the Pilgrim Fathers called Edward Winslow, of what has often, and inaccurately, been called the First Thanksgiving.

> Our corn [meaning wheat] did prove well, and God be praised, we had a good increase of Indian corn, and our

barley indifferent good, but our peas not worth the gathering, for we feared they were too late sown. They came up very well, and blossomed, but the sun parched them in the blossom. Our harvest being got in, our governor sent four men on fowling, that so we might after a special manner rejoice together after we had gathered the fruit of our labours. They four in one day killed as much fowl as with a little help beside, served the company almost a week. At which time, among other recreations, we exercised our arms, many of the Indians coming amongst us, amongst the rest their greatest king Massasoit, with some ninety men, whom for three days we entertained and feasted, and they went out and killed five deer, which they brought to the plantation and bestowed on then governor, and upon the captain and others. And although it be not always so plentiful as it was at this time with us, yet by the goodness of God, we are so far from want that we often wish you partakers of our plenty.[2]

The story, as Winslow tells it, is of a harvest-home celebration, of the kind familiar from centuries of observance in rural England, interrupted by the appearance of a force of Indians, intimidatingly larger than the surviving Pilgrims, but showing themselves friendly.

The other image is a visual one. It is a painting by the great *Saturday Evening Post* illustrator of the mid-twentieth century, Norman Rockwell. It is World War II, and a New England family watches happily as the turkey, roasted to perfection, is placed on the table.

It is not surprising that Thanksgiving has provided a theme for some of the very best American artists. Both Winslow Homer, perhaps the greatest of all American painters, and Thomas Nast, surely the most influential of American cartoonists, were fascinated by Thanksgiving in war and peace. Both returned again and

FREEDOM FROM WANT
(Printed by permission of the Norman Rockwell Family Agency)

again to one aspect or another of the holiday as custom or symbol. Homer, as a young man, painted *Thanksgiving Day in the Army: After Dinner the Wishbone* in 1864, while the Civil War was still raging, and a pair of wood engravings for *Harper's Weekly* in 1858:

Thanksgiving Day—The Dinner and the Dance. The German-born cartoonist, who was both radical and sentimental in the Victorian manner, drew several images of Thanksgiving, including one called *The Rich Man's Turkey, The Poor Man's Turkey* and a charming drawing, *Arrival Home*, showing the children being greeted by Ma, Pa, and the family dog. He also drew a powerful image of Lady Liberty on her knees, drawn for the first Thanksgiving Day ordained as a national feast at the crisis of the Civil War by Abraham Lincoln on November 26, 1863. The president, too, can be seen at prayer in Nast's drawing.

Over time artists' versions of the Thanksgiving story have naturally reflected changing preoccupations and assumptions, not to mention stereotypes. Indeed, around the end of the nineteenth and the beginning of the twentieth centuries, Thanksgiving paintings were close to being a genre, like those jocular pictures of Roman Catholic cardinals enjoying their dinner and their wine. The genre was unsteady in its understanding of history in general, and Native American history in particular. Jennie Augusta Brownscombe, in *Thanksgiving in Plymouth*, painted in 1925, showed only the white folks sitting at the table while Elder Brewster prayed and the Native Americans sat or stood well away from the feast. Another oil painting, by Edward Percy Moran, shows a Pilgrim in high boots and a steel helmet, attended by women in mobcaps, welcoming to a table heaped with food three warriors wearing the costume of nineteenth-century Plains Indians. As late as 1945, N. C. Wyeth, in *The Thanksgiving Feast*, showed women serving turkey to men at a long table where the solitary Native guest again wears, as if he were a Sioux rather than an Algonquian from New England, a feather in his headdress.

The iconic representation of Thanksgiving, however, the image that perhaps best captures the popular idea of the holiday and what it stands for, was Norman Rockwell's 1943 painting, *Freedom from Want*. Rockwell, an accomplished commercial artist, was also a talented painter, if in a style that now seems as dated as a seventeenth-century Dutch interior. He could dash off clever sketches of comedy or pathos on deadline, but cared so much about this work that it took him seven months to finish it to his satisfaction.

His theme was taken from President Franklin D. Roosevelt's famous Four Freedoms speech to Congress on January 6, 1941. It was still almost a year before the United States entered World War II, but the President was warning the American people of the danger from fascist dictatorships. "Every realist knows," he said, "that the democratic way of life is at this moment being directly assailed in every part of the world—assailed either by arms or by secret spreading of poisonous propaganda by those who seek to destroy unity and promote discord in nations that are still at peace." Skillfully linking this theme of the need for national unity to fight fascism with his own New Deal program of welfare state policies, Roosevelt listed the values on which Americans could agree. He was proposing, and Rockwell was portraying, the values Americans ought to be willing to fight for.

"We look forward," Roosevelt said, "to a world founded upon four essential human freedoms"—freedom of speech, freedom of worship, freedom from want, and freedom from fear—and he spelled out his vision of what it would mean, "in world terms," to secure those freedoms. Rockwell came up with powerful concrete images for each of Roosevelt's abstractions. He represented freedom of speech in the strong, prickly figure of a neighbor, a certain Jim Edgerton, dressed in leather blouson and work clothes. He is standing up in the town meeting in Arlington, Vermont, where Rockwell lived at the time, and putting forth unpopular ideas to a somewhat disapproving audience in business suits. Freedom of worship was illustrated by contrasting faces, old and young, in profile in the pale light of a church. Freedom from fear was evoked by the image of an American couple looking gently down at their tranquilly sleeping red-haired children. The mother is gently pulling the covers up over them, while the father holds in his hand a newspaper folded so that all that can be read of its headlines is: "COMMUNISTS KI . . . and "HORROR HIT . . . "

Freedom from Want captured the moment when Grandma, reaching across a smiling Grandpa, puts the roasted turkey on the table. Eleven family members, of all ages, are talking animatedly, and the bottom edge of the picture cuts the table, so the suggestion is both that there are more children at the foot of the table, and that the viewer, too, is invited to join the feast. Just as Rockwell is known to have felt uncomfortable that *Freedom from Fear* would suggest American complacency that American children were not at risk, so he told friends that he was afraid that *Freedom from Want* might be interpreted as excessive abundance. Perhaps that is why there is no wine or beer on the table, only tap water in plain glasses.

The "partakers in plenty" around the table, of course, are all white, cheerful, and healthy-looking. All are smiling. The three seated guests who are seen in full face—a vivid, youngish woman with dark hair on the right, balanced on the left by a man who could be her husband and an excited child—have the broadest smiles and the whitest teeth. Rockwell was a man with a strong social conscience, but this is the picture of a comfortable middle-class America. Indeed the model for Grandma was the Rockwell family's cook, Mrs. Thaddeus Wheaton. There is silver on the table, and fine china, and at the bottom of the picture a plate piled high with that age-old symbol of wealth, a cornucopia of fruit.

LIKE WINSLOW'S FEAST, ROCKWELL'S IS AN IMAGE OF PLENTY. The traditional menu is meant to suggest the food the Pilgrims ate at the First Thanksgiving: turkey and cranberry sauce, pumpkin pie, squash, and candied sweet potatoes. Historically, this is plain wrong. The Wampanoag Indians of coastal Massachusetts certainly ate squash in the early seventeenth century, with corn and beans, supplemented by venison and abundant seafood for protein; it was a key part of an excellent diet. They ate pumpkin, but not pumpkin pie. Early recipes treated pumpkins like apples, slicing them and frying the slices before placing them in a crust. But in 1621 the Pilgrims had neither the ingredients (butter and wheat flour) for piecrust, nor an oven to bake it in.

Some dishes that have pushed their way into the traditional canon would not have been on the Pilgrims' table simply because they did not grow in the cold, rocky soil of New England. Sweet potatoes were a southern contribution to American cooking, unknown in New England until much later. The same is true of pecan pie. The South did not celebrate Thanksgiving at all regularly until the nineteenth century, though curiously, given how closely the custom was associated with Yankee abolitionist piety, Jefferson Davis proclaimed Thanksgiving for the Confederacy before Lincoln did the same for the Union. There is no evidence that cranberries were served at the First Thanksgiving. Although cranberries are an important crop in Massachusetts—which today supplies about 30 percent of the nation's requirements, behind only Wisconsin—and acres of them still grow in the boggy ponds just inland from Plymouth, it would be fifty years before an English visitor mentioned that the locals were in the habit of boiling cranberries with sugar to make "a sauce to eat with meat." In 1621 there would certainly have been no sugar.

Most shocking of all, given the central part played by turkey in the modern mystique of the holiday, it is virtually certain that turkey was not served at the feast Winslow describes. It is unlikely that turkey was the fowl the Pilgrim hunters brought home. With their long, heavy matchlock muskets, cumbersomely muzzle-loaded and fired from a fixed rest, and even with their slightly more maneuverable fowling pieces, or "snapchances," the best they could do would have been to shoot geese or ducks sitting on the water.

Not that the Pilgrims were unfamiliar with turkey. They knew it, contrary to mythology, not from North America, but from England. The wild turkey (*Meleagris gallopavo*) was indeed originally an American species, but not a New England native. It was first introduced into Europe from Central America by the Spaniards in the 1520s. By the time the Pilgrims reached America it was already well known in England (as indeed was the pumpkin). They were called "turkeys" because they reached England from the Mediterranean, whose southern and eastern shores were then ruled by the Ottoman Empire. Probably they made the last stage on the journey to London on ships bringing the spices of the East that had arrived overland at ports in the Levant. (The French, likewise, called turkeys *dinde,* from *d'Inde,* meaning "from India.") By the 1550s, Archbishop Thomas Cranmer of Canterbury was telling the English clergy, in the interests of restraining gluttony, not to have more than one of a list of "great fowl," including turkeys, at any one meal. Half a century before the First Thanksgiving, turkey was familiar enough in the London markets that its price was officially regulated.

There were, however, no turkeys at Plymouth. James Deetz, a former senior staff member at the Plimoth Plantation museum in Plymouth, Massachusetts, has stated that the excavation of some ten sites at Plymouth yielded only one turkey bone. "We finally found some turkey bone after ten years of digging. The circumstantial evidence is that it wouldn't be very likely. Turkeys are very hard to kill and the matchlocks of the period weren't very good for hunting." Today, according to James G. Dixon of the U.S. Forest Service, the wild turkey, threatened with extinction two hundred years ago, has made a good recovery. But eastern Massachusetts is one of the few parts of the country where it is rarely found.

EDWARD WINSLOW
*(Photo courtesy of the Pilgrim Hall Museum, Plymouth, MA,
reprinted with permission)*

More to the point, it is plain from Winslow's account that the feast he describes was not really a Thanksgiving as the Pilgrims understood that word, even though Winslow, who might be called the first American booster, speaks of "our plenty." (In reality it was several years before the Pilgrims were free from the fear of hunger.) When he wrote, he was at pains to attract further English settlers by describing the good things to be found around Plymouth. "This bay is a most hopeful place," he wrote, "innumerable store of fowl, and excellent good, and . . . fish in their season, skate, cod, turbot, and herring . . . abundance of mussels the greatest and best that ever we saw, crabs and lobsters in their time infinite." He went on to list the fruit trees, cherries and plums and many others, the berries, herbs such as sorrel, watercress, and "great store of leeks and onions." But not turkey.

The gastronomic centerpiece of that First Thanksgiving, in any case, was supplied not by the Pilgrims but by the Wampanoag

Indians: it was they who produced five deer. To Englishmen of the Pilgrims' generation venison was an aristocratic dish, preserved by the king and his noblemen in their parks and chases. (Shakespeare himself is said, apocryphally, to have got into trouble as a young man by poaching the deer in Sir Thomas Lucy's park near Stratford.) Common folk could lose a hand or even their lives if they were caught poaching the king's deer. Winslow does not say how the deer was prepared. Probably it was cooked in a *sobaheg*, the Wampanoag word for stew, which the Native Americans of New England still make, or perhaps, if there were a hundred mouths to feed, in a whole series of *sobahegs*. Daniel Gookin's description of Indian life, written in 1674, suggests how a venison *sobaheg* might have been made.

> Their food is generally boiled maize or Indian corn, mixed with kidney beans, or sometimes without. Also they frequently boil in this pottage fish and flesh of all sorts, either taken fresh or newly dried . . . . These they cut in pieces, bones and all, and boil them. . . . Also they boil in this furmenty all sorts of flesh that they take in hunting, as venison, beaver, bear's flesh, moose, otters, raccoons . . . several sorts of roots, as Jerusalem artichokes, and ground nuts . . . and squashes.

Coon stew! An ambitious restaurateur today might well call it "special game casserole." The feast, if it was anything like the ones Gookin tasted, must have been a savory masterpiece. It was not a celebration of plenty, however. It was rather a kind of backwoods diplomatic encounter. As we shall see, both the Pilgrims and the Indians were nervous of one another in 1621, but they met because they needed one another. Winslow's feast was one of a whole series of meetings at which the English and the Wampanoags tried to establish good relations. In March 1621 the Pilgrims' Governor

John Carver even agreed something like a formal nonaggression pact with Massasoit, which simply means "the king" in the Wampanoag dialect of Algonquian. He sealed it with the best imitation he could put on of a formal meeting between two high potentates of baroque Europe, which included trumpeters, an exchange of kisses, and great draughts of strong liquor, which made the unaccustomed Indian sweat profusely.

The feast Edward Winslow described has come to be called the First Thanksgiving, and accounts from serious histories to commercial Web sites date the origins of Thanksgiving to the fall of 1621. Generations of Americans have been taught that the Thanksgiving meal of today not only celebrates that feast, shared with the Indians, but replicates its menu. It is clear that neither of these beliefs is true. There were no turkeys. Or cranberry sauce or pumpkin pies. Nor did the Pilgrim Fathers call themselves Pilgrims at the time, and strictly speaking they weren't Puritans either. And of course it is stretching a point to call them Americans: certainly they always referred to themselves as Englishmen.

What we are seeing, when we sit down to a Thanksgiving turkey, is a prime example of what historians have come to call "the invention of tradition." There is absolutely no harm in that. Indeed, Thanksgiving is one of the most innocent and happiest of American traditions. If it is not true, as the Italian proverb says, it is well invented. But, again, it was not invented all at once. It did not spring full grown from the imagination of a seventeenth-century Pilgrim Father.

The companions who splashed ashore some three-quarters of a mile through the freezing waters of Provincetown bay, and later threaded their way in a small dismasted boat and a snowstorm through the sandbanks of Plymouth harbor, had no grandiose plans. Theirs was, from one point of view, a modest enterprise. To see the compact they signed on board *Mayflower* as one of the founding charters of American democracy is to misunderstand both what they thought they were about, and their reasons for doing it. They set about building no more than a village, and what mattered to them was that they were gathering together a church, their church.

This apparently unexceptional ambition was, however, at once the culmination of centuries of European history, and the genesis of the distinctive American variant on that history. It all happened because a tiny band of friends from an obscure cluster of villages in one of the remoter corners of England believed that their God had called them to establish a church in their way, and refused to obey the worldly authority of king or bishops over their spiritual quest.

The Thanksgiving holiday does have ancient origins. Indeed, they go back long before Elder Brewster, William Bradford, and their friends ever saw the sandy beaches of Cape Cod. If at first it was not celebrated in the exact way that has become traditional, that is very appropriate. Thanksgiving is a festival that has adapted to changing circumstances through almost four centuries of American history, in ways that reflect interesting light on that history. The forms may have changed. But the ideals of gratitude, generosity, hope, and aspiration have been constant.

Almost every phase of American history has left its mark on the idea of Thanksgiving. The history of America's most beloved holiday is the history of much that is most innocent and generous in American history. The most beloved of America's festivals celebrates an achievement of true moral grandeur. The story of how a bare hundred men, women, and children landed on the unwelcoming shores of what came to be called New England, how they lost half their number to illness within a few months, and found themselves among a Native American population that was itself stricken by epidemic disease, is a story of heroic courage to rank with the greatest epics of antiquity. The Pilgrims, as I shall call them for the sake of simplicity, showed a mixture of sheer guts, good sense, and sober self-restraint that is wholly admirable.

EDWARD WINSLOW'S DESCRIPTION OF WHAT CAME TO BE
called the First Thanksgiving is the fuller of the only two eyewitness accounts that have survived of the feasting shared by the
newly arrived Pilgrim Fathers and their Native American neighbors. The other, shorter account is by William Bradford, one of
the Pilgrims' leaders and their historian. Winslow's version, which
Bradford used when he came to write his own history many years
later, comes from a book, published in London only two years after the Pilgrims landed in America, called *Mourt's Relation*. It is a
puzzling book in more than one respect. It purports to be an eyewitness report, for one thing, yet there was no one called Mourt
among the Pilgrims. Some historians believe that Mourt was short
for George Morton, who came out to Plymouth on the *Anne* in
1623. More likely it was a pseudonym, and the *Relation* was written
by several authors. Most of it, it is generally assumed, was probably
written by Edward Winslow himself, including the description
quoted above. He was a printer from Droitwich in Worcestershire
in the West of England, whose family claimed high and even royal
blood. He had worked with the Pilgrims' Elder, William Brewster,
setting up in type and printing religious books while the Pilgrims
were living in Holland. He became one of the most trusted and re-
liable, and incidentally one of the most prosperous, of the colony's
leaders, and served as governor after Bradford for many years. His
son, Josiah, succeeded him in that office.

It is clear that one of Winslow's motives was salesmanship: He
wanted to encourage more Englishmen to emigrate to Plymouth.
(The section of *Mourt's Relation* that contains the account of the
First Thanksgiving is called "A letter sent from New England to a
friend in these parts, setting forth a brief and true declaration of
the worth of that plantation; as also certain useful directions for

such as intend a voyage into those parts.") Not only does he gloss over the privations that had only recently killed half the original settlers, he even speaks up for the New England winter. "Some think it to be colder in winter," he says cautiously, meaning colder than in England, "but I cannot of experience so say." Four centuries later, winter in Massachusetts is far colder than in England. Winslow goes on to assure English readers that "men might live as contented here as in any part of the world." That may well be true, though the number of Yankees who moved west and south in search of better soil and warmer winters argues otherwise.

Another obstacle to the feast described by Winslow being the First Thanksgiving is that in general, the Pilgrims did not approve much of giving thanks to their God with feasting. They preferred fasting.

Protestants generally disapproved of the Roman Catholic church's elaborate calendar of holidays and saints' days. They saw it as part of the "superstition" they wanted to reform. The whole thrust of the Reformation was to get rid of the superstructure the church had added over the centuries to the evangelical simplicity. The Pilgrims observed only three holy days. They kept the Sabbath strictly once a week. And in special circumstances they held either Days of Prayer and Humiliation, when misfortunes suggested that God was displeased with them, and also Days of Thanksgiving, when, for example, an epidemic of illness was over, a ship arrived in the harbor with desperately needed supplies, or the harvest was saved.

Just such a day was held, just two years after the "First Thanksgiving." No rain fell for six weeks and both corn and beans were parched "as if they had been scorched before the fire." Edward Winslow himself reported that the crop failure, and the supposed wreck of a ship that was expected to bring provisions, moved the settlers to "humble ourselves together before the Lord by fasting and prayer." They met in church for "some eight or nine hours."

The next morning "soft, sweet and moderate showers of rain" fell and continued for two weeks, saving the crops, "mixed with such seasonable weather as it was hard to say whether our withered corn or drooping affections were most quickened or revived." And so, Winslow recorded, "another solemn day was set apart and appointed for that end, wherein we returned glory, honor and praise, with all thankfulness, to our good God, which dealt so graciously with us."[3]

This surely deserves to be celebrated as the first true Thanksgiving. But it is less susceptible to heroic mythmaking: A sober meeting to give thanks for the rain isn't as much fun as a feast. The earliest reference that can be found to anything like a Thanksgiving feast in the Pilgrim colony comes from John Lothrop, the minister in Scituate, fifteen years after the "First Thanksgiving." It is also the first suggestion that the holiday was seen as a time for the fortunate to help the less fortunate. On December 1, 1636, he recorded:

> In ye Meetinghouse, beginning some halfe an houre before nine and continued until after twelve a clocke, ye day being very cold, beginning with a short prayer, after that an other Psalme, then the Word taught, after that prayer and then a psalme. Then making merry to the creatures, the poorer sort being invited of the richer.[4]

There is a suggestion of inclusiveness here. But it involves the poorer sort among the English, not Native Americans.

The First Thanksgiving, in short, if it was a thanksgiving at all, was not exactly the thanksgiving that is commemorated in the fourth week of November in the twenty-first century. But thanksgiving, with a small *T*, for the year's crop and for deliverance from danger, was entirely familiar both to the Pilgrims and to the Wampanoag.

The Pilgrims remembered the English "harvest home," still celebrated in country parish churches today, and the Wampanoag were used to *Keepunumuk*, the traditional feast at the "time of harvest." Certainly Thanksgiving has part of its origins in the ancient and almost universal human custom of giving thanks for the year's crops and the blessings of the gods on fragile human societies.

Thanksgiving did begin to be celebrated more or less regularly in New England later in the century, often as "Forefathers' Day." Originally this was a matter for the church, but by the eighteenth century, both before and after the Revolution, it was sometimes ordered by government as an official celebration. Governor William Shirley of Virginia, for example, ordered a day of thanksgiving in 1749, to celebrate rain after a long drought. Governor William Pitkin of Connecticut did the same, more politically, after the repeal of the Stamp Act, and President George Washington ordered thanks to be given for "many blessings" in 1789 and again in 1795.

Three of the very greatest of American presidents, in fact, helped to establish Thanksgiving as a national holiday. It was Washington who first proclaimed it as a national American festival. It was Abraham Lincoln who yielded to the impassioned advocacy of the poet, editor, and doughty campaigner for women's education, Sarah Josepha Hale, and declared Thanksgiving a national holiday in 1863, at the height of the Civil War. And it was Franklin Roosevelt who annoyed half a nation when he moved its date, at the prompting of the retail leaders, so as not to conflict too closely with Christmas.

In 2002, Plimoth Plantation—the outdoor museum that vividly and with painstaking scholarship reproduces the Pilgrims' settlement a couple of miles down the road from its original site on the banks of the Town Brook in downtown Plymouth—put on an exhibition called *Thanksgiving: Memory, Myth and Meaning*.

Thanksgiving is indeed a myth, as well as a heart-warming celebration. Almost every generation of Americans has reinterpreted the thanksgiving story to fit in with its own values and beliefs. It meant one thing to colonial subjects of the English crown, and another to the citizens of the new Republic. During the long period of the Indian wars, indeed, it sometimes reflected fear and hostility towards Native Americans. A cartoon in the November 20, 1890, edition of *Life*, for example, called "The Thanksgiving of our Forefathers," shows the white New Englanders sitting peaceably in church while fierce Indian warriors pepper them with arrows through the windows. And that was at a time when attitudes towards Native Americans were already, if gradually, beginning become less antagonistic.

As New Englanders moved westward, first to the "Western Reserve" in Ohio and then across the broader Middle West, they took Thanksgiving with them. During the Civil War, southerners borrowed a national celebration from the "damn Yankees," and in the later nineteenth century the new immigrants from eastern and southern Europe, like the Irish and the Germans earlier in the century, fell in love with Thanksgiving as a symbol not only of American plenty, but also of American inclusiveness and American patriotism. As Norman Rockwell's powerful imagery shows, it fit the New Deal ideology perfectly. Franklin Roosevelt's political coalition depended on marrying together established American values and immigrant aspirations. Finally, since the 1960s, a new way of remembering Thanksgiving has reflected new sensitivities to race and gender, and at long last Native Americans, too, have reclaimed a place at table. Since 1970, the American Indian Movement has held a Day of Mourning in Plymouth every Thanksgiving Day. Since then, Plimoth Plantation has been careful to include exhibits of Indian life by reproducing the camp of Hobomock (or Hobbamock), the Pilgrims' Wampanoag neighbor and friend.

That alone makes the story of Thanksgiving a priceless thread in the weaving of American culture. But what is even more extraordinary is the sheer historical drama of the coming together of a few dozen Englishmen and no more than a few hundred Algonquian Indians on the coast of Massachusetts.

How did it come about that those particular Englishmen found themselves settled in fewer than a dozen frame dwellings astride the clear-running Town Brook, cautiously confronting fellow human beings who were so utterly different from themselves? Why did they cross the Atlantic, and how? And how exactly did their story bequeath to America the powerful myth of the Thanksgiving holiday? That is the story I will try to tell in this book, a story that marches forward to reflect the history of America, but also reaches so far back that it can be seen as the fulfillment and culmination of great movements in the history of Europe.

CHAPTER ONE

The Reformation

IN THE EARLY YEARS OF THE SIXTEENTH CENTURY, A hundred years before the Pilgrims set out from Holland to cross the Atlantic, Europe was being transformed by a whole series of convulsive, irreversible changes. Two in particular had a direct influence on the Pilgrims' adventure: the great revolution in religious belief and practice, which we call the Reformation, and the expansion of Europe into Africa, Asia, and the Americas that has been called "the great frontier."[1]

In 1517 the monk Martin Luther nailed to the door of the cathedral in Wittenberg in central Germany ninety-five "theses," or propositions, as we might call them. They denounced abuses in the administration of the church, contradicted much of its theology, and challenged its authority. Luther's act is generally taken as the symbolic beginning of the Reformation, which divided Europe politically and intellectually, and led to almost two centuries of bitter conflict, remorseless persecution, and war.

Luther's rebellion, however, was only one incident in a time of profound and disconcerting change that reached into almost every village and farm from the bloody frontier with the Ottoman Turks in the northern Balkans to the highlands of Scotland and Scandinavia, and from the Atlantic shore to the steppes of Russia. Decisive events rained down on the cities and countryside of the whole continent. In 1492 the Jews were banished from Spain by the Spanish king Ferdinand. In the same year the Genoese skipper, Christopher Columbus, working for the same monarch, landed on the island of Hispaniola in the Caribbean. Two years later the king of France invaded Italy, touching off fierce wars that threw the rich Italian city-states, the most advanced societies in Europe in many ways, into half a century of misery and chaos, while at the same time releasing some of the ideas and even the spirit of the Italian Renaissance in art and thought into northern Europe.

In the middle of the fifteenth century, Mehmet II, the Conqueror, had ridden his white horse into the space before the great Greek cathedral of Holy Wisdom and sprinkled his turban with dust in token of humility. He climbed to the roof, and, as he looked out over Istanbul, then the world's richest city, and the anchorage known as the Golden Horn, he recited a couplet about the fragility of empires:

> The spider serves a gatekeeper in the halls of Chosroes
> The owl calls the watches in the palace of Afrasyab.[2]

Soon the Conqueror had pushed the Turkish frontiers to the Euphrates in the east and to the Danube in the west. Christendom trembled with fear of Islam, and by the third decade of the sixteenth century fierce Muslim armies were campaigning in the heart of central Europe. The historian of Protestantism Diarmaid MacCulloch believes that "the fear that this Islamic aggression engendered in Europe was an essential background to the Reformation, convincing many on both sides that God's anger was poised to strike down the Christian world." Luther himself believed that the Turks were the agents of God's anger against sinful Christendom. MacCulloch says it is "impossible to understand the mood of sixteenth-century Europe without bearing in mind the deep anxiety inspired by the Ottoman empire."[3]

During those same years, too, Europe was on the move. The turmoil brought to the Mediterranean by the Turkish advance was shifting the balance of power west and north, first to Portugal and Spain, later to France, the Low Countries, and England. Portuguese explorers had ventured farther and farther down the coast of Africa. In 1488 Bartholomeu Dias reached the southern tip of Africa at the Cape of Good Hope, and in 1497 Vasco da Gama reached India and began to trade there, opening up the road to the Spice Islands and the fabulous wealth of China, which the Portuguese reached by 1513.

By the 1440s, European captains had joined in the slave trade, already started by African traders, many of them Muslims. In 1510 the first African slaves were shipped to the Caribbean.[4] By 1518, King Ferdinand of Spain had sent the first slaves to Hispaniola, the first of some eleven million to follow them.[5] They were all the more needed to work on plantations, in mines, and in many other jobs because Native American peoples were so grievously diminished by epidemic diseases brought by the Europeans that they could not be used instead.

As early as 1480, sailors from half a dozen North European countries had begun to visit the Dogger Bank and the coasts of Labrador, Newfoundland, and Maine to fish for cod and herring, and to hunt whales. The cod were so plentiful off Newfoundland that sailors could lower a bucket and pull it up full of fish. And although Pope Nicholas V, with the Bull *Romanus Pontifex* in 1454, and his successor Calixtus III, in *Inter Caetera* two years later, confirmed the monopoly of the Spanish in the Americas and the Portuguese in Africa (as well, by papal miscalculation, as in northeast Brazil), that cut no ice with the North Europeans. It was not long before French, English, and Dutch "interlopers," some with powerful and even royal backing, began to muscle in on the rich trade of the Indies in slaves, sugar, tobacco, silver, and gold.

The whole axis of European trade shifted. As it became more dangerous for Italian and other Western European merchants to trade with the Ottoman Empire, trade shifted from the Mediterranean to the Atlantic and the Indian Ocean. (It was no accident that the Genoese, including Columbus and Cabot, took so big a part in the new American trade; Genoa was cut off from the profits of its traditional Black Sea trade by the rise of the Ottoman Empire.) From Asia and the Caribbean, traders and sailors brought back new foods, new textiles, new diseases, and new ideas about the nature of the world.

The sheer size and diversity of the world the Europeans now "discovered" contradicted or challenged the rigid ideas of the medieval church about almost everything. Thoughtful Europeans were confronted by the idea that there were "more things in heaven and earth than are dreamed of" in medieval Christian philosophy. At the same time the onward march of the Ottoman Turks, who routed the armies of the king of Hungary and his Christian allies at Mohacs, and invested Vienna nine years after Luther posted his theses, seemed to threaten the very survival of Christendom in Europe.

Nothing was more important to the Europeans of this exciting and dangerous early modern world than their religion. And nothing was threatened with more profound change. The fundamental difference between the Roman Catholic Church and its Protestant critics was that the Catholics gave primacy to the authority of the church itself, as interpreted by the papacy, the bishops, and the learned. The Protestants preferred the authority of scripture as interpreted by individual conscience. But the Protestants were soon divided among themselves.

The most important and lasting rift was between the followers of Luther and those who later adopted the doctrines of John

Calvin, who left the University of Paris and moved (by way of Basel) to Geneva in 1536. Calvin taught that men and women were predestined to salvation or damnation, to heaven or to hell. Although it was Luther who first unleashed the pent-up energy of revolutionary change, the Protestant faith that had the most impact in England and Scotland, and which specifically inspired the Pilgrims, came more from Calvin than from Luther.

We can't understand who the Pilgrims were, and why they left England to settle first in Holland and then on the unwelcoming shores of Cape Cod Bay, unless we delve a certain way into the history of the Reformation and of the religious ideas and the religious politics of the England they left.[6]

In the sixteenth and early seventeenth centuries, all Europe, from Bohemia to Scotland and Ireland, and from Poland and Sweden to Spain and Portugal, was consumed with the great quarrel between the Reformation and the Catholic Church. At first, the Reformation seemed to be winning. But from the 1550s the Roman Catholic Church, upheld by the House of Hapsburg, the greatest power in Europe, fought back with its own movement: the Counter-Reformation.

The Reformation, like any great movement of ideas, had many causes. It sprang from anger at the way Holy Church was seen to have been corrupted in the late Middle Ages by political intrigue and priestly greed. One issue among many others touched off the Lutheran rebellion: the church's (relatively recent) doctrine of purgatory and the idea that spiritual salesmen, known as "pardoners," could enable Christians to buy remission from the pains of purgatory after their death. The final straw was the campaign to raise money to build the great basilica of St. Peter's in Rome: It was the pardoners fanning out across Germany to raise money to repay the loans made to the pope to rebuild St. Peter's by the great Augsburg banking house of the Fuggers that were the immediate cause of Luther's rebellion.[7]

The Reformation's causes, of course, were both deeper and wider than that. It reflected the inchoate, frustrated energies of people in a civilization that was being stirred to its depths by the new learning, by daring explorations in Africa and Asia as well as across the Atlantic, and by the inflationary impact of the great discoveries of gold and especially silver in Spanish America, not to mention the fear and loathing inspired by the syphilis epidemic that was probably another import from the New World.[8] Certainly the sufferings of syphilis patients were all too evident in the streets of early fifteenth-century European towns.

In some places the Reformation appealed to new social classes—merchants, capitalists, townsmen, but also artisans and the urban poor—who felt excluded or oppressed by the established, and allied, orders of the church and the nobility. There was widespread anger at the wealth and in many instances the moral corruption of the church. In some parts of Europe, the new religious ideas gave expression to old, long-buried feelings of national identity or to memories of oppression. The Czechs, for example, turned to Protestantism because of their memories of their fifteenth-century reformer and martyr Jan Hus, while Protestantism flourished especially in those parts of southern France that had not forgotten either the savage persecution of the Cathar heretics centuries earlier or the more recent atrocities committed by the king of France's Catholic agents in the south.

There was not one Reformation, in fact, but many. Lutherans fought with Calvinists, and both savagely persecuted Anabaptists and others they saw as heretics. One idea united them: the passionate conviction that Christ's gospel had been hidden and perverted, not just in recent decades, but for centuries, by the hierarchies of the Church and especially by the Papacy, and that the only cure lay in a return to the uncorrupted Christianity of the Bible and most especially of the New Testament.

After a first round of destructive religious wars, starting with the "Peasants War" in Germany in the 1520s, which threatened church and secular rulers as well, it had been agreed by the Peace of Augsburg in 1555 that the people of each state must obey the religion of its ruler: *Cuius regio, eius religio,* "whose rule, his religion."[9] It was not until the Treaty of Westphalia, though, almost a century of bloody warfare later, that the same toleration was allowed to Calvinist governments as to Lutheran evangelicals.

The Reformation developed differently in the various nations of Europe. Spain and Italy were relatively little affected. (Italy at first more than Spain, where the Inquisition, long before the Reformation, had developed ruthlessly effective techniques for sniffing out and punishing heresy in its struggle to rid the Peninsula of all traces of Jewish and Muslim belief. But in Italy, too, by the time the Pilgrims landed at Plymouth, the Papacy, led by Camillo Borghese as Pope Paul V, had reestablished a firm hold on society and belief.) In France, after initial successes and decades of brutal wars of religion, the Reformation was finally defeated by royal power. Henry IV, the Protestant champion, converted to Catholicism, famously proclaiming that "Paris is worth a Mass." Many French Protestants, the Huguenots, were driven into exile in Holland and England.

Germany was divided. Its divisions would eventually erupt, in the second decade of the seventeenth century, into the savagely destructive Thirty Years War. But from the middle of the sixteenth century, the Counter-Reformation of the Roman Church, backed by the imperial House of Hapsburg and by the new, utterly dedicated Jesuits, converted back to Catholicism many principalities and provinces and even rich cities like Vienna, Munich, and Prague that had wavered in their faith.

To the east, the Reformation made inroads at first in the vast lands of the Jagiellon dynasty, lords of the Polish kingdom, and the Grand Duchy of Lithuania. For several decades these lands were notable for their toleration, a "state without stakes." But in 1587 a prince of the Swedish royal house, whose mother was a Jagiellon, became king of Poland as Sigismond III and converted Poland to Catholicism. His attempt to do the same in Sweden, backed by a papal nuncio and the Jesuits, failed, and Scandinavia has remained staunchly Protestant. In Hungary, too, the Reformation took root for a time, and after the Turkish victories of the mid-sixteenth century the principality of Transylvania joined the Protestant camp. But by the end of the seventeenth century, the Hapsburgs fastened Hungary securely back into their Catholic dominions.

The Low Countries—the modern Belgium and the Netherlands—were divided geographically. To the south, many rich provinces remained Catholic under the often ruthless repression of the Hapsburg sovereigns and their lieutenants. The Spanish viceroy, the duke of Alva and his "council of blood," earned a fearsome reputation for bigotry and cruelty by persecuting Protestants ruthlessly with torture, cruel executions, and even massacres. But in the northern Netherlands, Holland and the United Provinces rebelled and eventually won their religious and political freedom. Many Jewish refugees from Spain and Huguenot Protestants from France found shelter there and contributed to Holland's brilliant century of intellectual and economic success.

In Britain, too, the impact of the new ideas was complex. In England, Protestant ideas were strong in the East and the great mercantile city of London, but Catholic belief survived strongly in remoter parts of the North and West. In Ireland, the native Irish remained loyal to the old religion, but English landlords and later settlers, many of them from Scotland, brought with them a fierce brand of Protestantism. In Scotland, the religious division put Presbyterians and Calvinists in opposition to the Stuart kings and to the Catholic Mary, Queen of Scots.

Everywhere, religion was inextricably bound up with political quarrels and international politics. English kings and queens persecuted Catholics, for example, not only because they believed the

Catholic religion was in error, but because they saw Catholics as the agents of powerful and frightening rival states, Catholic Spain and France. Queen Elizabeth even offered amnesty to Jesuits who were willing to acknowledge her authority.[10] Few were tolerant about religion in the sixteenth or the seventeenth century: religion was just too important. The salvation of souls and the survival of dynasties both depended on it.

THE PILGRIMS WERE NOT FROM HOLLAND OR GERMANY OR Bohemia, or even Scotland. They were English, and the strange story that ended by depositing them in what became Massachusetts cannot be understood except as a consequence of the particular circumstances of the Reformation in England.

For English Protestants, as for their coreligionists elsewhere, and especially for the more radical Protestants known as Puritans and Separatists, the Bible, as interpreted by the individual conscience, was the only authority they acknowledged.[11] In England, Protestant ideas arrived early from the European continent, seeding in a soil prepared by followers of the preacher John Wycliffe, known as Lollards, and their protests against the church a hundred years earlier. It was not until the 1530s, when Henry VIII, for mixed reasons, determined to divorce his Catholic wife, Catherine of Aragon, and marry first Anne Boleyn and then four other women, that the religious quarrel became mixed up in both national and international politics.

Henry VIII of England insisted that England should be a Protestant country and made himself the head of the Church in England, partly because he wanted to divorce his wife and because he needed a male heir, partly because he wanted to consolidate England as a European power—independent of the power of the king of France and of the House of Hapsburg, rulers of Austria, Hungary, the Low Countries, Spain, and much of Italy. He was tempted, too, by the vast wealth he could command by suppressing the monasteries and distributing their lands, and by the political power he would win by distributing part of these properties to ambitious families so as to attach them to the Protestant cause. Almost five hundred years later, many of the great landed families of England owe their fortunes to grants of monastic lands and still inhabit monasteries rebuilt as palaces: the Herberts, for example, at what was once the Benedictine abbey of Wilton and the Russells at Woburn Abbey.

Henry's heir, Edward VI, the son of Jane Seymour, was a very bright but sickly child who had been brought up by Henry's last queen, Katharine Parr, to be a Protestant. But he was only nine when he assumed the throne and died just six years later, to be succeeded by Henry's daughter, Mary, who had remained a loyal Catholic and did everything she could to return England to its Catholic loyalty. Mild in other respects, she persecuted Protestants without pity. In three years some three hundred men and women were burned at the stake as heretics for their Protestant beliefs. One of them was the archbishop of Canterbury, Thomas Cranmer, author of the majestic language of the Church of England's Book of Common Prayer. Two other bishops were burned with him in Oxford. Most of the victims of the Marian persecution were ordinary folk, plain men who were staunch enough to suffer for their beliefs and for their hope of eternal life. Their sufferings were recorded in the gruesome bestseller of the century, John Foxe's *Book of Martyrs*.[12] It was a work of propaganda genius, and it was cherished by the Pilgrims and other English Protestants with an affection second only to that given to the Bible itself.

Mary's persecution was hated even by English men and women without any strong Protestant sympathies. That alone, it has been said, made it certain that England would in the end be a Protestant country. When the Protestant Bishop Ridley, about to be burned at the stake in Oxford, encouraged his fellow sufferers by saying they should be of good cheer for they had lit a candle that would not be put out, he spoke the truth. But Mary did something else that did even more to guarantee the failure of her efforts to turn back the Reformation. An insecure woman approaching middle age, she wanted to marry, and of all the princes of Europe she chose to marry the king of Spain, Philip II, the man most English people saw as their most dangerous enemy. He was the son of the great Hapsburg emperor, Charles V, and the heir to his possessions in Europe and America, probably the greatest fortune any European ever owned between Charlemagne and Napoleon. He also inherited Charles's ambition, and even more that of Philip's uncle, the emperor Ferdinand: to utterly destroy the Reformation. The marriage was a disaster. After the wedding in Winchester Cathedral Philip spent little time with Mary. He ended up at war with England, a war that rewarded him with the humiliating destruction of his fleet, the Spanish Armada.

Henry VIII's other daughter, Elizabeth, was made of very different stuff. She had the body of a feeble woman, as she told her troops on the eve of the sea battles against the Armada, yet she had the stomach of a man. She was determined to avoid the mistakes both of her father the Protestant persecutor, who ended up, in spite of his brilliant talents, as a paranoid sadist, and of her half sister Mary, the Catholic fanatic. Her own personal beliefs may have been close to those of the Catholics: She had an altar with candles in her private chapel royal. But from the moment she arrived on the throne, it was clear that some form of Protestant religion would have official approval. The Elizabethan settlement was already planned by officials close to Elizabeth, notably William Cecil and Nicholas Bacon. The key documents were already drafted.

Gradually, however, disappointment spread among the more zealous Protestants. The first open disagreement was over the vestments prescribed for the minister in the communion service, which struck Protestants as suspiciously popish. Already in the 1560s there was a distinct Protestant party in the church and the country, led by favored courtiers like Cecil and the earl of Leicester. In the 1570s the Protestant party was alarmed by the threat from Rome. In 1570 two powerful northern landowners, the earls of Northumberland and Westmoreland, raised a rebellion in the North—where the Catholic religion was still cherished—which was ruthlessly suppressed, and two years later the leading Catholic noble, the duke of Norfolk, was executed on suspicion of treason.

In 1570, to encourage Catholic rebellion, Pope Pius V made the catastrophic tactical mistake of excommunicating the English monarch, which absolved her Catholic subjects from the duty of allegiance they owed her. The religious conflict in England—from then on if it had not been before—was a political struggle between the Queen of England and the papacy, along with its protectors in the House of Hapsburg; Elizabeth had no intention of losing it. If she had not been committed to the Protestant side before, she was now, and with her stood the majority of the English people. By the end of her reign, although individual Catholic loyalty survived, England had become institutionally a Protestant country, and so, for the most part, had Scotland. The history of Ireland was to be very different.

The English Catholics had set up seminaries, at Douai in the Spanish Netherlands and elsewhere on the other side of the English Channel, from which Jesuit missionaries went to make secret Catholic converts and from time to time to encourage rebellion. Some 180 of these brave men, and some of their English hosts and helpers, were caught, and executed in barbaric ways. Only a few years before the Pilgrims emigrated to Holland, the Catholic conspirators in the "gunpowder plot," an attempt to blow up Parliament, were mercilessly tortured and executed. But Jesuit priests and Catholic recusants were executed as much for political reasons, because they were seen as agents of the national enemy, Spain, as for their religion.

The purpose of Elizabeth's very considerable statecraft was to give England a settlement that would avoid the religious wars that were devastating France and Holland and would cripple Germany after her death. In that way she meant to preserve her crown and to leave a united kingdom, free from French or Spanish domination, to her dynasty. Although she had no heirs, in the wider sense she was decisively successful.

The strategy of the Elizabethan settlement was to preserve a doctrinal balance between traditional Catholic practice and the new ideas of the Reformation, while maintaining the English monarch's control of the church.[13] The "Anglican" Church of England set up by Elizabeth was a compromise. It took over much, though by no means all, Catholic doctrine. It retained bishops and claimed apostolic succession for them and for its priests.[14] But theologically it accepted the central tenets of the Reformation. It rejected the "real presence" of the body and blood of Christ in the Mass, which it renamed the communion service.[15] It accepted, though in practice it did not emphasize, the central Calvinist belief in the predestination of souls to salvation or damnation. Its services were in English, not Latin, and it still replaced the authority of the pope over the Church of England with that of the monarch.

The instruments Elizabeth used were two acts she persuaded Parliament to pass in 1559, intended to heal the wounds left by the Reformation and Mary's attempt to reverse it. The Act of Uniformity made church attendance compulsory and required all churches to use the Book of Common Prayer. There were some concessions to Catholics: the wording of the communion service was left vague and church furnishings were to be left intact. The Act of Supremacy made the queen Supreme Governor of the Church of England.

In designing her settlement, Elizabeth was fighting on two fronts. The more obviously dangerous threat came from the Catholic Church, supported by the French monarchy and, even more formidably, by the Hapsburg empire, led by Philip II. On the other hand, Elizabeth was also determined that her church must not lean too far in the opposite direction, towards the more extreme Protestant doctrines. For one thing, she saw such ideas as another threat to her own royal authority. She also saw it as likely to create the very religious divisions and conflicts she was above all anxious to prevent. Many of the more unyielding Protestants had fled to Holland, Germany, or Switzerland to escape the persecution under Mary. The very day after the news arrived in Strasbourg, Basel, and Geneva that Mary was dead, the leading English Protestant refugees there set off for home. These returned exiles were from the start the core of a Protestant movement, and several of them became the bishops entrusted with imposing the settlement. But Elizabeth was not prepared to allow this group to dictate their views to her,[16] though her most trusted and influential minister, William Cecil, Lord Burghley, was a strong if discreet supporter of the Protestant cause. Throughout her reign, while the great majority of the clergy accepted her settlement, an influential minority of the most fervent and popular preachers, the most learned scholars and the most admired leaders in the church saw it as no better than a shabby compromise with that anti-Christ, the Roman pope.

The Elizabethan Settlement, therefore, was a shrewd set of compromises aimed at establishing a national church with the monarch at its head. What she had in mind, one continental Protestant charged, was a papacy with herself as pope. It did not at first engage the enthusiasm of many people. Only two religions were recognized in most places in England, Diarmaid MacCulloch has written,[17] and neither of them was Anglican: there were Catholics, and there were Protestants. But that was to change. By the time the Pilgrims left England, the Catholics were largely discredited by their association with foreign nations, and English nationalism was beginning to rally Englishmen round the national church.

For much of Elizabeth's reign, many English Protestants had felt that the Elizabethan Settlement did not go far enough to embrace the ideas of the Reformation. Most of these understandably decided to avoid trouble and possible persecution by remaining within the Church of England, attending its services and obeying its new rules. These people, and they were numerous and influential, including in particular many of the powerful merchants of London and not a few wealthy landowning families,[18] were known as Puritans. There were gradations among them. Some wanted the church to move more, others less, in adopting the beliefs and the liturgy of the Reformation.

As Elizabeth's long reign went on, a second generation of Protestants became impatient with the slow pace of change. Many clergy and educated laymen were frustrated by the way the bishops imposed what seemed to them to be popish practices. They were attracted by the Calvinist version of Protestantism, by the Geneva Bible, and by the idea of replacing the authority of bishops by the presbyterian system of church government.

Most, even of these "precise," "puritan," or "godly" Protestants, remained more or less comfortably inside the Church of England. Indeed, in the new century, the Anglican church would begin to develop a strong religious personality of its own—quite distinct from Catholicism. So in the later years of Elizabeth's reign, and under her successor James I, most "Puritans" remained inside the Church of England, however unhappy they might be with its liturgy and theology, if only because they were not ready to risk persecution for their interpretation of Protestantism.

The Pilgrims, therefore, were not Puritans, because that name was used to describe those among the stronger Protestants who remained inside the national church. Only a few brave souls felt so vehemently about their beliefs that they were willing to risk punishment and persecution by defying the church's rules. They were given, and gave themselves, various names. Often they referred to themselves as "the godly." Sometimes they were called, especially by their enemies, Brownists, after Robert Browne, a Cambridge Presbyterian who formed a Separatist congregation. (Presbyterians believed that the Church, as in Calvin's teaching, should be ruled not by the monarch or by bishops, but by "presbyters," or ministers, who would have absolute control of doctrine, ritual, and public morals.)[19] Sometimes they were called Anabaptists, the name used to discredit the most radical Protestants in Germany and Holland. But the commonest name for them was Separatists. A few congregations in London and elsewhere defied the church authorities and maintained separatist beliefs.

Robert Browne was a pupil at Cambridge University of Thomas Cartwright, a more formidable figure, and now acknowledged as a founder by Presbyterians.[20] Cartwright was a brilliant academic and a charismatic preacher, but he fell foul of John Whitgift, his superior at the university and later archbishop of Canterbury. He fled to the Protestant court of the elector palatine at Heidelberg on the Rhine, and although he was allowed to return to England, he was put on trial for heresy and imprisoned. But punishing one ex-professor with strong Protestant beliefs did not change anything. Many, especially in Cambridge but also in London and in the cloth-working villages and towns of East Anglia, thought what only Cartwright and a few other bold spirits had dared to say. Cambridge was a hotbed of the more extreme Protestant ideas, and as we shall see the Pilgrim leaders were both directly and indirectly influenced by Cambridge Separatism.

By the late 1580s, with the authorities nervous about the possibility of a Spanish invasion and on the lookout for conspiracy and treason, the Separatist church in London was being hard pressed by the government. By 1593, fifty-two members of the congregation had been sent to prison, where some of them died of jail fever.

In April two Separatist leaders, Henry Barrow and John Greenwood, were hanged, and in May John Penry, reputed to be the author of the disrespectful attacks on the bishops known as the "Martin Marprelate tracts," was also hanged.

Leadership of the persecuted Separatists in London fell to Francis Johnson, another Cambridge graduate. He and his brother, George, and two others set out for Canada, where they promised to "greatly annoy that bloody and persecuting Spaniard," something they would have found hard, given that the nearest Spaniards were almost two thousand miles to the south in Florida. The Johnson brothers were shipwrecked in the English Channel and found their way to Amsterdam, where an English Separatist church in exile had emigrated with the tacit approval of the English authorities. In 1569 the Dutch Parliament, the States-General, decided to allow freedom of conscience to both the Reformed and the Catholic churches. In 1578 the city of Amsterdam, the biggest and richest city in the Netherlands, went further and allowed freedom of worship for all, even for Anabaptists, hitherto persecuted almost everywhere.[21]

The Johnson brothers fell out because Francis—so his brother George maintained—was "blinded, bewitched and besotted" by his wife Thomasine, a "bouncing girl who wore whalebones in her breast, an excessive deal of lace, and a showish hat."[22] So the English Separatists in Holland, the "Ancient Church," as they came to be known, were soon bogged down in church disputes, scandal, and personal feuding. But Holland, at war with Catholic Spain, had already become established as a place of refuge for Protestants of many different shades of opinion. By the end of Queen Elizabeth's reign, the more outspoken Protestants were in a precarious situation, and several hundred of them had fled over the narrow seas to Holland.

Queen Elizabeth died on March 24, 1603. Everyone knew she would be succeeded by her rather remote relative, James VI of

Scotland, who would become James I of England. (He was the great-grandson of Henry VII of England.) But no one knew how James would behave as king of England, and in particular no one had any clear idea how he would behave in relation to religion and to the Elizabethan Settlement. James's mother, the tragic Mary, Queen of Scots, was the daughter of the Scottish king James V and his wife, Mary, a member of the powerful French Catholic noble family, the Guises. She was put to death by Elizabeth, not without years of provocation, because she acted as the focus and figurehead of a long series of Catholic plots, actual or alleged.

So as James rode slowly southwards down the Great North Road from Edinburgh to London to take over his kingdom, stopping from time to time to hunt the deer, all religious parties waited with some nervousness to see how he would declare his policy. Some English Catholics hoped that James, because of his Catholic mother, might turn out to be their friend. Puritans and Separatists in England also looked to James in hope. After all, he was theoretically a Calvinist in doctrine. He was certainly the ruler of a country whose national church was Presbyterian. Two Catholic plots against his life were discovered in the first months after he became king, and within a year the Jesuits were ordered to leave the country. As the new king, clever, learned, and neurotic, reached London, he was handed the Millenary Petition, signed by a thousand Puritan clergy, urging him to reform the Church and in particular to require of the clergy only that they should obey the royal supremacy and acts of Parliament.

Little did they realize that James smarted from what he felt was the humiliation of his treatment at the hands of the Scots Presbyterians, and in particular at those of Andrew Melville, regarded as the greatest preacher in Scotland since John Knox. Melville had publicly grabbed the king's sleeve, a horrible offence in itself in an age when kings and queens were seen as almost divine, and called him "God's silly [simple] vassal." "There are two kings and two kingdoms in Scotland," Melville went on. "There is Christ Jesus the King and his kingdom the Kirk, whose subject James VI is, and of whose kingdom he is not a king, nor a lord, nor a head, but a member." James did not like that. He didn't intend to tolerate any such behavior in his new realm.

Less than a year after becoming king of England, James summoned a conference at Hampton Court, the great palace Henry VIII had built on the Thames west of London. On Saturday, January 14,[23] he first met the bishops and told them that he had disliked the opinions of the Puritans since the age of ten. Two days later he saw the bishops again, this time with four leaders of the Puritan party.[24] He told them he intended to have in his kingdom "one doctrine and one discipline, one religion in substance and ceremony." More than once he muttered his slogan: "No bishop, no king!" When the Puritans asked him about Presbyterianism, he lost his temper. Presbytery, he snapped, "agreeth with monarchy as well as God with the devil. Then Jack and Tom, Will and Dick shall meet and at their pleasure censure both me and my council." At which he left, muttering that he would "make them conform, or he would harry them out of the land, or else do worse!"[25]

At a final meeting the Protestant divines, bravely, spoke up for Puritan ministers in Lancashire and elsewhere for whom it might be dangerous to preach the official doctrine. Before the bishops could answer, James cut in and accused his critics, with an unfairness that revealed his mind all too clearly, of putting their private interests before "the general peace of the Church."

Separatists, and indeed Puritan Protestants within the Church of England, had been warned. James was not their friend. They must conform, or expect persecution.

CHAPTER TWO

Scrooby

They shook off this yoke of antichristian bondage,
and as the Lord's free people joined themselves
(by a covenant of the Lord) into a church estate,
in the fellowship of the gospel,
to walk in all His ways made known . . .

—WILLIAM BRADFORD, *Of Plymouth Plantation*

JUST AFTER HALFWAY ON HIS JOURNEY AS HE RODE SOUTH to become king of England, James, king of Scotland, passed what had once been an important stopping place on the road. This was the manor house of Scrooby. It lay, and lies, at a place where the three counties of Nottinghamshire, Lincolnshire, and Yorkshire meet, in flat country, on a little stream called the Idle, which flows not far away into the broad river Trent. To the west lie the Pennine hills, the spine of England, and to the east a long ridge crowned by the great cathedral church of Lincoln. The immediate neighborhood is good farming country, with Sherwood Forest not far to the south. To the north in the early seventeenth century it was still fenland, now drained, but then marshes that were the haunt of wild geese, ducks, bitterns, and plentiful deer.

It was here, in this unremarkable and often muddy corner of the English Midlands, that the core group came together who were to lead the Pilgrims to the New World. Seventy years or so after the Reformation reached England and captured the English Church thanks to Henry VIII's decision to divorce his Catholic queen, provincial England had hardly changed since the Middle Ages. Even after the great upheavals of the 1540s and the 1570s, much of the North still owed loyalty, and paid rent, to great princely families such as the Percys, earls of Northumberland, the Nevilles, earls of Westmoreland, the Cliffords in the Yorkshire Dales, and to great princes of the church, chief among them the bishop of Durham and the archbishop of York.

Nearer London, the new money made in trade and manufacturing, in the City and in foreign ventures, at the Bar and at Court, had begun to find safe investment and social status by investing in land, diluting the power of the old nobility. It had not yet reached these wild and conservative northern counties. New ideas, the ideas of the Reformation, were beginning to arrive, but they had not yet changed a social structure that was still essentially medieval. There were the great landowners and their tenants and their servants. There were smaller landowners, yeomen, struggling to bash a decent living from the soil. There were a few others, no more than a handful in each parish: a parish priest, one or two shopkeepers, a handful of craftsmen, none much better off than peasant farmers. The rest were cottagers and, at the bottom of the whole pyramid, landless laborers and "lusty rogues." It was a hard society, brutal in its punishments, but just: Each man knew his rights, and the law protected them. For the most part it was tied to the slow cycle of the farming year, but it was also a world of deep religious faith, now being shaken by passionate arguments about theology and liturgy, the Bible and the church, God and man. More than most European societies by 1600, Englishmen were literate. Between them, Will Shakespeare the Warwickshire butcher's son, John Bunyan, son of a Bedfordshire tinker, and the learned Cambridge clergymen who wrote the King James's Bible were creating the English language for all to read. Englishmen cherished their rights. They read their Bible. And they sought salvation. They were quick to quarrel and slow to back down. Some of them were ready to run great risks, on the seven seas and among dangerous enemies, to make their temporal fortunes. Others faced even the risk of death, on the gallows or at the stake, for their spiritual beliefs. In the past two generations, a world that had not changed much for centuries had suddenly started to change very fast indeed.

There was historical irony about the fact that vast transformations should have come to a head in the quiet manor of Scrooby. It was harassment from the local ecclesiastical authority, namely the archbishop of York, that drove the little church of Scrooby villagers to look for toleration abroad. Yet the leader of that church owed his livelihood and his family's modest local prominence to the same source. The estate of Scrooby had belonged for centuries to the archbishops of York, whose diocese stretched even farther south, thirty miles or so the beautiful church of Southwell.[1] The archbishop's house at Scrooby had once been a palace, with more than forty rooms, worthy to receive a prince of the church and his entourage on their travels, but by the seventeenth century much of it had been demolished. It was still a staging post on the Great North Road, and the home of the archbishop's steward, who was also the king's postmaster. Scrooby was one of twenty-five post offices on the 294 miles between London and Berwick-on-Tweed, the frontier town between England and Scotland.[2] And it was still a substantial place, with its brew house, bake house, barns, and stables around what was left of the archbishop's house.

The Great North Road hardly deserved its romantic name. In many places it was no more than a wide strip of muddy ruts. It was still an important artery at a time when travel by land was slow as well as dangerous. A traveler might have met noisy cattle being coaxed to market by drovers, peddlers with their packs of pins, needles, threads, and notions, well-escorted ladies in ponderous coaches, and merchants on horseback. Queen Elizabeth had ordered the road to be cleared of trees and brush for 200 feet on either side of the track as some protection against highwaymen. The mounted post was expected to travel at seven miles an hour in the summer, but only five miles an hour in the winter. The king's postmaster was supposed to keep three good horses and rent them out for one-and-a-half pennies a mile, as well as supplying good leather bags, lined with cotton or baize, and keeping proper records. The man carrying the post had to blow his horn whenever he met travelers, when passing through a town, and three times an hour in open country, which suggests that it was not crowded. But the road was an important artery just the same. Along it traveled the king's messengers as well as private travelers, and in time of war armies passed that way.

For the weighty responsibility of looking after one short stretch of the royal road, the postmaster was well paid by the standards of the time. When King James came to the throne the postmaster's wages went up from twenty to twenty-four pence a day. And he could supplement that salary by running the post office as a kind of inn for travelers.

More than a quarter of a century before Queen Elizabeth died, a certain William Brewster was appointed "bailiff and receiver," that is, estate manager, by the archbishop of York for his manor of Scrooby, and not long afterwards he was also appointed as the royal postmaster. Brewster was a "gentleman," that is, a man of good family, entitled to his own coat of arms, but not a member of the nobility. The second archbishop of York he served, Edwin

Sandys, was to be a patron and friend to the whole Brewster family, and the archbishop's son, a second Edwin, played a vital part in the Scrooby migration to America.

Postmaster Brewster's son, another William, was born in 1567. He grew up in the spacious remains of the old archbishop's palace. When he was only thirteen he went to study at Peterhouse, the oldest college in the University of Cambridge. The life was frugal, with a quarter-penny piece of beef and porridge twice a day. The day began with divine service in Little St. Mary's Church at 5 A.M., and the students worked hard. They were expected to study the *trivium*, the first and easier part of the medieval course of the seven liberal arts, namely grammar, rhetoric, and logic, and to attend lectures by the professor of divinity, and "readers," or scholars, of Greek and Hebrew.

There were many brilliant minds at work in Cambridge when young Brewster arrived there, including Francis Bacon, lawyer, essayist, and scholar, and William Shakespeare's closest rival, Christopher Marlowe. William Gilbert, author of the first great book of scientific research published in England, *On the Magnet*, was a fellow of St. John's College, Cambridge, and William Harvey, who discovered the circulation of the blood, was a Cambridge doctor of medicine. It was a group of mainly Cambridge scholars of Brewster's generation who between 1607 and 1611 completed the magnificent Authorized Version of scripture, known as King James's Bible.

The dominant intellectual fashion in Cambridge, ever since the ideas of the Reformation first arrived in England from Europe, was Protestantism, and in particular the more radical ideas of those who became the English Separatists.

We know from the books in Brewster's library later in life, as well as from what we know of his declared opinions, how deeply he was influenced by Protestant ideas. At the heart of them was the conviction that the Protestant Reformation had not been carried far enough, that the Elizabethan Settlement was a cowardly political compromise, and that the church must go further in the direction of reform if it was to be purged of the corruptions and distortions introduced by the medieval period, with its papacy and its bishops, its ceremonial and vestments, its hierarchy and its worldly wealth.

Victorian scholarship, anxious to support the Elizabethan compromises that created the Anglican settlement, minimized the issues that were at stake in the Reformation. It was not simply a movement to reform the relatively recent corruptions and backslidings of the Catholic Church, as exemplified in the sale of indulgences or the wealth and worldliness of prelates. It was a challenge to the whole authority of the Church, to its virtues as well as its vices. The great cause could all too easily get bogged down in arid disputation or furious disagreement over liturgical detail, and often did. But its central call was for a daring and essentially new idea: that each individual human being must be responsible for his or her own soul.

The theological ferment of the sixteenth century could and did drive good and clever men to injustice and even war over a word or a sign or even a piece of priestly clothing. But that did not mean that the quarrels were either trivial or pointless. At first the English Puritans concentrated their attack on the Prayer Book of 1559, which had preserved many Catholic traditions in the outward rituals and practices of the church. They objected to the wearing of priest's vestments such as copes and surplices, to kneeling to receive Holy Communion, to the keeping of fast days and holy days, and to the giving of the ring in marriage. They were even unhappy about celebrating Christmas and Easter and the other great traditional feasts of the church, which they saw as a medieval corruption of apostolic simplicity.

Later they broadened their attack so as to question the whole organization and governance of the church. Nowhere was this more the case than at Cambridge. It may be that the university's location in the east of England, close to the Low Countries, or the contacts due to the wool trade, tilted Cambridge towards the Protestant faith. Again, Cambridge was not far from London, where foreign contacts and foreign doctrines were common. At any rate, quite early in Elizabeth's reign some leading Cambridge academics petitioned the Queen's minister, William Burghley, who was sympathetic to the Protestant cause, asking to be allowed not to wear surplices, a loose white cotton garment worn by priests and seen as a relic of Catholicism, because "here were a multitude of pious and learned men who thought in their consciences all using of such garments was unlawful for them." In the early years of Elizabeth's reign there had been "a concerted effort to purge the university and the town of the remnants of popery."[3] The university's processional cross was sold, and so too were copes, surplices, mass books, and chalices. The colleges began to use the Geneva Psalter, so that Cambridge fellows and undergraduates were singing the music of John Calvin's Reformation church.

Thomas Cartwright, who was given one of the most prestigious chairs in the university in 1569, was deprived of it in the following year because of his opinions, and fled to Geneva to avoid imprisonment. When a year after that two London clergymen published an Admonition to Parliament attacking the Anglican compromise in almost every particular, Cartwright wrote a *Second Admonition*, defending them. His position was attacked in turn by Richard Hooker, the great High Church theologian, in the most magisterial apologia the Church of England has ever produced, his *Treatise on the Laws of Ecclesiastical Polity*. At Cambridge, Cartwright fell foul of John Whitgift, who was successively master of Trinity, where Cartwright was a fellow, Queen's professor of divinity when Cartwright was Lady Margaret professor, and eventually archbishop of Canterbury. Cartwright was subsequently regarded as the father of the Presbyterian tradition. His personal rivalry with Whitgift had much to do with his later career and so with the future of Presbyterianism in Britain and America.

It was only in a third and most radical phase, however, that some of the boldest minds despaired entirely of reforming the church from the inside, and again many of the most influential were living in Cambridge. They advocated leaving the national church to set up congregations where the members would constitute a "priesthood of believers." After four centuries of religious diversity within Protestantism, it is now hard for us to imagine how daring this was. Americans are used to choosing between dozens of churches. For sixteenth-century Englishmen, it meant abandoning the traditional belief that the church was one and indivisible, the body of Christ. Some of the most brilliant and most serious of William Brewster's contemporaries did just this. They went further than the earlier Puritans and advocated Separatism. One of them was Robert Browne, who resigned his living in Cambridge while Brewster was still in residence there. The three Separatist martyrs, John Greenwood, Henry Barrow, and John Penry, were all Brewster's contemporaries at Cambridge, and so was John Udall, who was imprisoned and condemned to death, but died before the sentence could be carried out. Cambridge, in fact, when young William Brewster from Scrooby arrived to study there, had been a hive of radical and perilous religious ideas for a generation, and those ideas were becoming more radical, and more perilous.

Brewster left Cambridge without taking a degree, which was common in those days for those not planning to become priests. Instead, through family or perhaps Cambridge contacts, he went to court and found employment as a very junior member of Queen Elizabeth's diplomatic service. He went to work for William Davison, Elizabeth's ambassador to the Netherlands, and later her secretary of state. Davison, according to Bradford, "esteemed him rather as a son than as a servant," and trusted him with matters of "greatest trust and secrecy."[4]

Brewster was being thrust in his teens into some of the most delicate and dangerous business of a dangerous age. In 1581 the great Dutch Protestant leader, William the Silent, head of the House of Orange, was murdered by an assassin paid with Spanish gold—part of Philip II's attempt to stamp out Protestantism, which was reaching its climax. Philip's greatest commander, the victorious duke of Parma, was ordered to destroy the Dutch resistance and with it the strongest bastion of the Protestant religion in all Europe at the time.

Elizabeth's diplomatic skill was taxed to the utmost. She understood that the best place to defend England against Spanish conquest was on the other side of the narrow seas. She feared that if she committed herself too far her armies would be destroyed and England's defenses stripped away. She was cautious both by temperament and because of the ferocious swings of fortune she had witnessed and experienced as a child. She decided to help the Dutch but not to commit her own or her kingdom's fortunes to them irrevocably. Davison had been sent on missions three times before to assure the Dutch of English support. In 1585 he went again, accompanying the Queen's former favorite and perhaps lover, the earl of Leicester, and he took young Brewster with him. Elizabeth's offer was to send five thousand infantry and one thousand cavalry to help the Dutch, but as security she demanded the keys to two fortresses until the Dutch had paid the cost of the expeditionary force. For one night Brewster actually slept with the keys of Flushing under his pillow.

Davison disastrously lost favor with Elizabeth when, after the Babington plotters' tortured testimony had implicated Mary, Queen of Scots, he refused to follow Elizabeth's suggestion that Mary not be put on trial for her part in the conspiracies, but should be secretly murdered instead. Davison, as an honest and wise adviser, could not agree, and doomed his own career by his refusal. Elizabeth finally signed the death warrant, and it was

Davison who took it to her ministers, Burghley and Walsingham. On January 8, 1586, Mary, Queen of Scots, was beheaded at Fotheringay Castle in the English Midlands. But the very day after signing the death warrant, Elizabeth repented, or simply changed her mind, and blamed Davison. He was disgraced, arrested, and sent to the Tower of London. Under interrogation, he protected the queen's reputation by not mentioning her suggestions that Mary be murdered. Even so, in March 1587, Davison was tried in the prerogative court of Star Chamber, fined a huge sum, and imprisoned during the queen's pleasure.

Brewster continued to serve Davison for a time after the latter's fall from grace. But his prospects at court were finished. In 1590, his father died and he expected to succeed him as postmaster at Scrooby. He learned that the postmaster general, Sir John Stanhope, had given the job to a friend of one of his relatives. Only through the intercession of the disgraced Davison and the far more effective support of the Queen's most powerful minister, William Cecil, Lord Burghley, was Stanhope put under pressure to revoke his decision and to give the postmastership at Scrooby to Brewster after all. So the young man was back at home in the Midland mud, having received a short but advanced education in the morals of courts and the trustworthiness of princes.

Even if courtiers and generals occasionally hurried up the Great North Road through Scrooby, it was a quiet, rustic corner. (It still is. The inn is now called *The Pilgrim Fathers*.) The local clergy were negligent and ignorant when they were not openly scandalous.[5] Oddly enough, perhaps just because this was such a neglected corner of the English countryside, it had a reputation for being one of the districts where Catholic loyalties lingered on.[6] But as James I came to the throne, making it ominously plain that he intended to make life difficult for the more radical Protestants, a sprinkling of clergymen with Cambridge connections and Separatist beliefs had settled in the area.

At Gainsborough, a river port on the Trent, the Reverend John Smyth had a rare opportunity to preach the Separatist doctrine with relative immunity. In the center of the now run-down little town lies one of the most magnificent of surviving medieval domestic buildings in all England, an imposing structure of stone, brick, and timber that occupies a whole city block.[7] Gainsborough Old Hall was built by a fifteenth-century aristocrat, Sir Thomas Burgh, reputedly to entertain King Richard III, the sinister Crouchback of Shakespeare's play, infamous for having had the two child princes smothered in the Tower of London. The Burghs, noble but impoverished, were forced to sell to a London merchant, whose descendant, Anthony Hickman, was a Puritan. It was he who allowed John Smyth to preach the Puritan creed in the privacy of his great hall. Smyth was a pupil at Cambridge of Francis Johnson, who had already fled to Holland by the time of James I's accession to the throne. In 1602 Smyth was in Lincoln, and already in trouble as a "factious man." One of his disciples was John Robinson, who was to be one of the three key figures in the Pilgrim story.

Another Cambridge Separatist, Richard Clyfton, a Derbyshire man and Cambridge graduate, was the rector of the little village of Babworth, a small community a few miles south of Scrooby on the fringes of Sherwood Forest, its church to this day tucked into the woods. Over fifty years old in 1606, with a "great white beard," Clyfton was appointed pastor to the congregation William Brewster had gathered round himself at Scrooby, "a grave and reverend preacher, who by his pains and diligence had done much good."

John Robinson, born in 1576 not far from Scrooby, was elected a fellow of Corpus Christi College, Cambridge, and later became a minister at a church in Norwich. But in 1604 Archbishop Bancroft of Canterbury, newly appointed by James I and a known scourge of Puritans,[8] had demanded that all clergymen must subscribe to every one of the Church's Thirty-Nine Articles. Robinson was one of the ninety ministers who refused and were therefore dismissed.[9] He retired to his birthplace, the village of Stourton-le-Steeple, and there married Bridget White, who herself had been born only half a mile away.

In about 1606, on William Brewster's initiative, the church at Scrooby was formally organized as a separatist congregation, with Richard Clyfton, newly expelled from his living as rector of Babworth, as pastor, and John Robinson as his assistant. Brewster was the Elder. Two years later, as King James's archbishops and their bishops began to demand obedience to the official church, Brewster and others were fined twenty pounds, a substantial sum in those days.

So in the early years of the seventeenth century the kernel of the group who were to become the Pilgrim Fathers who emigrated to found Plymouth was to be found in this unpromising cluster of villages in the English Midlands. William Brewster, the postmaster and former royal servant, and John Robinson, the Cambridge theologian barred from the Anglican clergy for his Separatist views, were two of the key trio of the Pilgrim leadership. The third was William Bradford, destined to succeed Brewster as the Pilgrims' leader, and to be their first and greatest historian.

Bradford was more than twenty years younger than Brewster and fourteen years younger than Robinson. He was born in modest prosperity in Austerfield, a village or small town just north across the county boundary into Yorkshire. He was the third child and eldest son of another William Bradford, who was described as a yeoman farmer. His mother, Alice Hanson, was the daughter of the village shopkeeper. His father died when he was only a year old. His mother married again, and William was brought up by his grandfather and uncles. By the time he was twelve, he was already a regular reader of the Geneva Bible, the version preferred by the stronger Protestants, and it was not long before he began to walk to Scrooby for prayer and lengthy discussion of religious questions at Brewster's home. When Richard Clyfton and John Robinson, under the aegis of William Brewster as Elder, organized their congregation in Scrooby, Bradford became a regular member, to the "wrath of his uncles" and the "scoff of his neighbors."[10]

The essence of the Separatist belief was that each congregation should seek its own salvation, and so not be bound by the Church of England's rules and regulations in matters of doctrine and discipline. In 1606, when the little church in Scrooby began to set out on that road, that was already a dangerous thing to do. When Bradford, many years after the Pilgrims had emigrated to North America, sat down to begin his history, he compared the sufferings of his Separatist friends to those of the early Christians and of the Protestants martyred under Mary. In this he exaggerated. No Separatists were executed under James, and however roughly James threatened the radical Protestants at the Hampton Court conference, he did not torture or execute them. Still, their future looked dark. James's bishops were keen to demonstrate their loyalty and the zeal with which they would pursue heretical belief. And they had legal power to do so. Brewster and two others were heavily fined and threatened with imprisonment. Bradford was right that "they could not long continue in any peaceable condition, but were hunted and persecuted on every side . . . some were taken and clapped up in prison, others had their houses beset and watched day and night. . . . [A]nd most were fain to flee."

By the fall of 1607, not much more than a year after the Scrooby congregation was founded, Brewster and his friends decided they had no alternative but to leave. They did not go because of persecution, or even the fear of persecution, but because it was plain that Tobias Matthew, the new archbishop of York, was determined to destroy their church. For them the supreme purpose, which they believed to have been ordained by God, was to keep their congregation together as a church to worship God in their own way.

Matthew was a subtle persecutor. He was careful not to create martyrs. But he was nonetheless relentless in his determination to destroy the Separatists. On his first visit to the district as archbishop he preached in nearby Bawtry church against Brownism. In November 1607, Gervase Neville of Scrooby was imprisoned for four months for heretical views. On December 1 it was Brewster's turn. He and another Scrooby layman were summoned to appear before the Court of High Commission and fined twenty pounds in their absence. Again the next April Brewster was summoned to the archbishop's beautiful church at Southwell and once again fined twenty pounds in absentia.

By this time Brewster was virtually an outlaw. He had already resigned his postmastership in preparation for flight. Those of the congregation who owned their own houses were secretly selling them. The obvious place to go was Holland, which had been a refuge for victims of religious persecution in England since the middle of the previous century. But in England, under a statute more than two hundred years old, as in many other places in Europe, you needed a license to leave the realm, and that license would not easily be given either to Roman Catholics or to dissenting Protestants.

The move would have to be secret. Brewster found a ship's captain who was willing to take them from Boston, a small port on the north side of the wide bay known as the Wash, and about 100 miles from Holland across the North Sea. They were able to reach Boston inconspicuously by taking a circuitous cross-country route, almost one hundred miles long, by water. They drifted down the little River Idle, which runs through Scrooby, to the Trent, then sailed up the Trent as far as Torksey, where an ancient canal, the Foss Dyke, built by the Romans, still curves gracefully through the flatlands to the Brailsford Pool, the broad inland basin below the hill of Lincoln. From there they could sail down the River Witham to Boston.

In Boston, however, disaster struck. Their captain betrayed them to the authorities. The local constables "rifled and ransacked them, searching to their shirts for money, yea even the women further than became modesty."[11] The magistrates were more sympathetic. Boston was a Puritan town. (The local vicar, John Cotton, sailed to Massachusetts in 1633 where his family became famous divines, and so did a number of other leading citizens.) But the magistrates still had to go through the motions of carrying out the law. The entire Scrooby party, perhaps about fifty to sixty men, women, and children, were imprisoned for a month. Brewster, Clyfton, Robinson, and four other leaders were sent for trial at the assizes in Lincoln, but were eventually released on bail.

It was a miserable situation. They had left their homes (most of them were tenants) and sold their furniture. Money and other possessions, including part of Brewster's library, had been stolen. They had no alternative but to try again.

The second time around, Brewster engaged a Dutch captain, and divided the party into two.[12] This time the women and children went by river again, but although they got there first, when the tide went out their boat stuck fast in the mud. The men, meanwhile, had been making for Killingholme overland. They marched there—a journey of more than forty miles—and were walking up and down on the bank waiting for the tide to lift the women's boat off when the captain persuaded them to go on board his ship. Suddenly he saw "a great company, both horse and foot, coming with bills [woodmen's blades used as battle-axes] and guns and other weapons, for the country was raised to take them." The men saw their wives and families arrested, but they were carried away on the wind and the tide. A fierce storm blew up, and the ship was driven almost to the coast of Norway, 400 miles across the North Sea, but—by God's providence, as they firmly believed—they eventually landed safely in Amsterdam—then, as now, the most important city of the Netherlands.

Brewster and Robinson bravely stayed behind and were arrested with the women, but once again the magistrates were embarrassed. The women and children were passed on from one jurisdiction to another. In the end, the authorities had the sense to let them go. Brewster and Robinson seem to have been allowed to go, too, and sailed unimpeded to Amsterdam. John Smyth, their Separatist neighbor from Gainsborough, with some of his congregation, had arrived there before them. So, finally, the church from little Scrooby was reunited in the wealthiest and most cosmopolitan city in Europe.

The Scrooby congregation might have been rustics, but they were not the sort of people to be easily deterred. When the storm was at its height, Bradford recorded, "and the water ran into their mouths and ears and the mariners cried out 'We sink! We sink!' they cried . . . 'Yet Lord Thou canst save!'"[13] And saved they were, for a great and godly adventure.

CHAPTER THREE

The Waters of Exile

AMSTERDAM, WHERE THE SCROOBY CONGREGATION NOW found themselves, was the New York of the seventeenth century. It was commercial, cosmopolitan, busy, and rich. It is said that in the early years of the century five hundred ships left its harbor every week, trading to the Baltic, the Mediterranean, the Hudson, the Spice Islands, South Africa, Japan—anywhere, indeed, where a profit was to be made. Money was being made faster than anywhere else in Europe, from land drainage and speculation, from shipping and trading, from importing wines and spices, from fishing and textiles. It was spent on paintings, china, elegant houses, and exquisite furniture, and also on oceans of alcohol, clouds of tobacco, and riotous nightlife.[1] Immigrants flooded in: Flemish fleeing Spanish rule in the southern Low Countries, French Huguenots, Jews whose grandparents had been expelled from Spain and Portugal, and among so many others a little colony of some four hundred English Protestant refugees. The city's population doubled in the last decade of the sixteenth century, and doubled again in the first ten years of the new century, to something over 250,000.

The Scrooby Pilgrims had arrived in what they must have expected to be a pious refuge, only to find themselves in the midst of the myriad worldly temptations of the wealthiest and most self-indulgent boomtown in Europe at the first apex of its opulence. For pious farmers and farmhands from a quiet corner of rustic England, Amsterdam was noisy, disconcerting, and immoral.[2] It could also be a hard place for those without money.

There were three English Protestant congregations there: the Ancient Church, also known as the Ancient Brethren, led by Francis Johnson and made up of English Separatist refugees; the *Begijnhof*, or English Reformed Church, a long-established Presbyterian church that served English and Scots merchants; and the Gainsborough brethren under John Smyth, who had arrived shortly before the migrants from Scrooby. The Ancient Church was going through the upheavals mentioned above, due among other causes to quarrels over what some saw as the immodest dress of some of the women members. Later, there were frank charges of sexual misconduct.[3] It was not plain how the Scrooby folk, most of whom spoke no Dutch (Bradford called it a "strange and uncouth language," though after a time he taught himself to speak it well enough to be understood) were going to earn their living in the big city. Bradford said, "they saw the grim and grisly face of poverty coming upon them like an armed man . . . from whom they could not fly." After less than a year in this modern Babylon, Brewster and his friends moved on, to the second city of the United Provinces, what Bradford called the "fair and beautiful city" of Leiden.

Leiden remains a beautiful city, home of one of Europe's greatest universities, with handsome houses reflected in the city's curving canals. In the early seventeenth century it was also a bustling place, with about 45,000 inhabitants in 1622, a focus of debates and conflicts of European importance. A generation before, in 1574, Leiden had earned its glory by its citizens' heroic conduct in the siege by the Spaniards, which lasted more than four months. To this day the city commemorates its deliverance from the great siege with a riotous fair. It was a close-run salvation: about one-third of the population died in the siege of starvation or the plague. In the end the Dutch opened the dykes and flooded the countryside so that their navy could get at the besiegers with its heavy guns and raised the siege.

William of Orange rewarded the city by establishing there the first Protestant university in Europe, its proud purpose to serve the freedom of the Netherlands as a bastion of the Reformation, though both Catholic and Jewish students were admitted, and in the late sixteenth century four-fifths of the students came from abroad. Later in the century the great philosophers René Descartes and Benedict de Spinoza were both to be found working there. Already by the time the Pilgrims arrived it was famous for its distinguished scholars like Justus Lipsius and Joseph Scaliger and the great theorist of international law, Hugo Grotius, not to mention its great library and its pioneering botanical garden. The painter Jan Steyn lived in Leiden, and when the Pilgrims arrived Rembrandt van Rijn, as a child of three, was living there, and later went to the Latin school in the very neighborhood where Brewster and his friends settled, clustered round the tall St. Peter's Church.

Here too the Scrooby congregation found it hard to make a decent living. Many highly skilled textile workers from the southern Netherlands had come to Leiden as refugees from the Spaniards, and the country folk from Scrooby could simply not match their skills. Many of them found work in the less skilled sectors of the textile industry, as "*say*" workers (*say* was a relatively coarse woolen fabric), glovers, wool combers and carders, twine makers, and hatters. One or two manufactured clay pipes. William Bradford, who married Dorothy May, a sixteen-year-old girl he had met from the Ancient Church in Amsterdam, earned his living weaving fustian, a high-quality kind of corduroy made from a mixture of fine wool and linen. William Brewster, helped by the trained printer Edward Winslow, set up as a typesetter and printer in the Stincksteeg,[4] or smelly alley, just off the Koorsteeg, Choir Alley, leading out of the square surrounding St. Peter's Church, the most imposing in the city, next to the ancient castle of the counts of Holland.

A few yards away was John Robinson's house in the Kloksteeg, the Green Close (de Groene Poort), with behind it a patch of land on which a dozen cottages were later built for needy Pilgrim families. Here was where the Pilgrim church met, in part of the Faliede Bagijnhof, a large building belonging to the university that was also used as a library, an anatomy theater, and a fencing school.

We know something about the religious services that were the reason for the Scrooby congregation's existence and for its removal to Holland. In the Protestant liturgy of the time, prayer and the Eucharist took second place to preaching and the exegesis of the Bible. There were two services every Sunday.[5] The first began early in the morning and would last altogether for about four hours, the congregation standing throughout. (Men and women worshipped separately, following ancient Jewish practice. They stood on opposite sides of the aisle.) The service would begin with prayer led by Pastor Robinson, extempore and guided by no book but by the Holy Spirit. Then lessons were read from the Geneva Bible and explained. Next the congregation sang psalms, unaccompanied, as musical instruments were forbidden as sinful, or at least Catholic, by Reformation teaching. Only then would Robinson preach, which he did for as long as two hours. On some but not all Sundays, Holy Communion would then follow, and baptism if there were new members to induct into the congregation.

In the afternoon the church would gather again for what was called "prophesying." This was not what was later called "speaking with tongues," but debate and discussion of a passage in scripture, in which the whole congregation were encouraged to take part, the unlettered as well as the learned. This second service, too, could last for three or four hours.

Although for the congregation as a whole life was hard, some of the Scrooby congregation prospered modestly. William Bradford and Brewster's oldest son, Jonathan, were among those who became *poorters*, meaning formal citizens, of the city, an honor that had to be earned and also paid for. The congregation, however, kept itself to itself. In Holland, marriage was a civil, not a religious ceremony, a tradition the Pilgrims took with them to New England. Marriage records show that the overwhelming majority of the English in Leiden married other English men or women.

At the time the Pilgrims arrived in Holland the Calvinist community there was being torn apart by a ferocious theological quarrel between the strict Calvinists, who argued for predestination of the elect and the damnation of the rest, and the Arminians. The term came to have a special meaning in England later, meaning the followers of Archbishop Laud, supporters of a High Church, proroyalist interpretation of the Elizabethan tradition under King Charles I. But in Leiden, when the Pilgrims were there, it meant the followers of Jacobus Harmenszoon, or Arminius,[6] who argued the more compassionate case that Christ had died on the cross for all men, and that God wanted all human beings to be saved. The Arminians, also called Remonstrants, believed that men and women possessed free will, and that all believers would be saved.

The controversy was bitter. It led to a public declaration at the Synod of Dort that Arminian belief was heresy and ended in rioting and a coup d'état. The patriotic statesman Johan van Oldenbarnefeldt, who had been the trusted ally of successive leaders of the Dutch rebellion against Spain, William the Silent, and Maurice of Nassau, took the Arminian side. He was arrested and beheaded after a scandalously unfair trial. John Robinson, now a student at the university, was persuaded to enter this fierce argument, in which he took the side of the strict Calvinists, and opposed the Arminian doctrines.

Meanwhile William Brewster found himself in more serious trouble. The books he was printing and publishing in the Stincksteeg were making a serious political stink in Britain. One of them, called the *Perth Assembly*, written by a Scots divine called David Calderwood, was a violent attack on James I and his bishops for attempting to impose episcopacy on the Presbyterian Scots church. The manuscript was smuggled out of Scotland, set up in type by Brewster, and the unbound books were then smuggled back in the false bottoms of French wine barrels. King James took personal offense. The book was denounced as an "atrocious and seditious libel," and the king ordered his ambassador in Holland, Sir Dudley Carleton, to find Brewster and bring him to justice. The authorities in Leiden seem to have done their best to protect Brewster. The English ambassador's officers failed to catch him, and he went into hiding in a village near Leiden. One of his helpers returned to England, published more seditious pamphlets, and ended up doing fourteen years in prison for his pains.

The king of England's bloodhounds continued to search for Brewster for months in Holland. However, he was no longer, as they thought, skulking in Leidersdorp, his first suburban hideaway. Instead, he had returned to London, beginning the patient negotiations that would be necessary if his band of followers were to make the bold move they were now contemplating.

THINKING BACKWARD, IT IS NATURAL TO THINK OF THE Pilgrim colony at Plymouth as just the second English venture in America, after Jamestown, as indeed it was. Some also remember the "lost colony," planted by Sir Walter Raleigh in 1587. But it is a mistake to see these events as so many isolated episodes. To the contrary, they were the fulfillment of half a century of effort, and they were also the expression of essentially Protestant ambitions. Dreams of colonies beyond the Atlantic were at the heart of the English fantasy in the Elizabethan and early Stuart era. (Shakespeare's patron, the earl of Southampton, was involved in transatlantic ventures, and his last play, *The Tempest*, reflects the fascination the ocean voyages had for him and his contemporaries.) For fifty years, for the whole of William Brewster's life, voyages of exploration and plans for "plantations," or colonies, in North America had seized the English imagination. For diplomatic reasons, Queen Elizabeth I could not always avow the extent of her involvement in backing some of these ventures. But she was personally and also financially committed to a strategy that would either flout the Spanish monopoly in the Indies, or succeed in an end run around the Spanish colonies by discovering a route either northwest past the northern coast of Canada, or northeast past Siberia.

Long before a single English colony had been settled on the American coast, indeed, America had been central to the strategic thinking of Elizabeth and her ministers. The young sea captains and adventurers—Humphrey Gilbert and his brothers, Walter Raleigh and Francis Drake, John Hawkins, Martin Frobisher and Richard Grenville—were her favorites, until they forfeited her favor for one reason or another. The great men of her court, too, Sir William Cecil, Sir Francis Walsingham, and Sir Christopher Hatton, all found it wise to stake a share in the voyages, and sometimes regretted the losses it cost them.

The conflict over the Spanish monopoly in America has been called one of the two great issues of the second half of Elizabeth's reign. It was inextricably linked to the other, the great conflict between the Protestant Reformation and the Catholic Counter-

Reformation. Indeed, the two were seen by Englishmen, and especially by English Protestants, as one single question: Would Spain, which after 1580 had conquered Portugal, so that the Pope's grant to Spain and Portugal had become what seemed to Englishmen a monstrous gift of boundless wealth to the Hapsburg family, be allowed to exclude Protestant Englishmen, Dutchmen, and—until the Huguenots were finally defeated in France—Protestant Frenchmen, from their rightful share in the bounty of America?

The English claimed that it was an Englishman (or rather an Italian in the service of the English king), John Cabot of Bristol, in 1497, who first planted their flag on the American mainland, when Columbus and the Spaniards were still conquering the islands of the Caribbean. Elizabethan Englishmen such as John Dee, the mathematician and astrologer who advised the queen, and the great champions of "western planting," Richard Hakluyt and his continuator Samuel Purchas, never tired of denouncing the Spanish claims. Because the Spanish monarchy had put itself in the service of the Counter-Reformation, sworn to extirpate the Protestant heresy, moreover, the whole project of ousting Spain from its monopoly of American wealth, was a strategic as well as economic Protestant ambition. However profoundly William Brewster and his friends might be at odds with James I's bishops and their views on church governance and ceremony, they were completely in sympathy with the Elizabethan tradition of "singeing the king of Spain's beard." It would be quite wrong to read back into their early-seventeenth-century minds the anticolonial or even the antimonarchical spirit of the late-eighteenth-century Founding Fathers. They were at once separatists and English patriots—in fact, nationalists abroad.

By 1617 THE LEIDEN CONGREGATION, LED BY JOHN ROBINSON and William Brewster, had come to the conclusion that they must leave Holland and emigrate to the New World that was opening up at that very moment in history. They were helped to come to that conclusion by a man who was to be at once a crucial ally and a thorough nuisance. This was Thomas Weston, a wealthy London ironmonger and adventurer (that is, investor), whose business took him to Holland. He and his associates had in fact been brought before the Privy Council in London and ordered to stop trading with the Netherlands in breach of the monopoly in the Dutch trade granted to the official Merchant Adventurers. Weston was keen to break into the North American trade and settled in America for a time, first in Virginia, then after adventures (in both senses) in New England, in Maryland. He was bold and entrepreneurial and also unscrupulous and he got into trouble with the law in Virginia as well as in Holland and in England.

Weston was willing and able to advance the Pilgrims the substantial capital they would need to establish themselves in America, and he always protested his love for them. But he was to be a thorn in their flesh. He tried to whittle down the share of the profits that went to those who actually made the journey to America, in favor of himself and his fellow passive investors. He constantly interfered in the colony's affairs, and tried to set up a rival to it. When his rival establishment collapsed, the Pilgrims, understandably with some reluctance, had to feed Weston's colonists out of their own still-scanty means to keep them alive.

So from the start there were two aspects to the Pilgrims' venture. It was primarily a religious movement, in search of the freedom to practice their own particular Protestant version of Christianity without interference from king or bishops. But it was also necessarily a business venture, obliged to earn enough to repay large loans from Weston and the other investors, something in practice they could only do by trading, especially for furs, with the

Indians. Those we call the Pilgrims, who actually migrated to America, were known as "planters," meaning settlers. Their financial backers were called the "adventurers."

Why did the Pilgrims decide to leave Holland and take their chances with an Atlantic voyage, Indians, disease, and hunger that had already destroyed or nearly destroyed earlier ventures at Roanoke, at Jamestown, and elsewhere? (The Jamestown colony was almost wiped out by an Indian massacre in 1622.)

William Bradford, looking back on the decision long afterward, when the Pilgrims had succeeded, in the sense that they had established their colony at Plymouth, but when it was already plain that it would be outstripped by the bigger, wealthier settlement at Massachusetts Bay, listed half a dozen reasons why they left Leiden.

The first was, quite simply, that life was hard for them there. That in itself might not have been enough to make them decide to emigrate a second time. The leaders and most of the others were tough and utterly dedicated people. What worried them was that, just because life was so hard, new recruits who might otherwise have come to salvation by joining what the Pilgrims saw as God's chosen church might be deterred. Then, too, they felt they were getting old. Within a few years, they would be in danger of what, as the leaders of a "gathered church," they most feared. They might be scattered or diluted. They were especially worried about their children. They were afraid of the example of the hard-working but fun-loving Dutch and what they saw as the "licentiousness" and "temptations" of the place. Already some of the younger generation had already got into dangerous courses. Some became soldiers, other sailors, and others succumbed to "dissoluteness and the danger of their souls." The straitlaced Pilgrims were particularly shocked that the Dutch, however strong their Protestant faith, did not keep the Sabbath. Once they had been to church on a Sunday morning, they felt free to enjoy themselves.

Then, too, the Pilgrims felt themselves to be English. They did not want their children to become foreigners, talking a foreign language. Their fears were not unfounded. The children of those Pilgrims who did not emigrate to New England, and they were a majority of the Leiden church, became completely assimilated to the Dutch by 1660.[7] The Pilgrims, of course, did not see themselves as becoming Americans. There was no such thing at the time. To emigrate to America was their way of remaining English.

Almost as an afterthought, Bradford added that they had great hopes of advancing the gospel in "those vast and unpeopled countries of America, which are fruitful and fit for habitation, being devoid of all civil inhabitants, where there are only savage and brutish men which range up and down, little otherwise than the wild beasts." From the start, there was a certain ambiguity. They saw the Native Americans as fellow humans whom they hoped to convert to the way of Christ; yet they also saw them as little better than wild animals, and that "caused many fears and doubts among them."

There was another danger to be feared if they stayed in Holland. In 1609 the savage war between Holland and Spain had been stopped by a twelve-year truce that was on the verge of running out. In central Europe the terrible Thirty Years War had already broken out. It would convulse Europe, killing millions by battle, massacre, and pestilence. It ruined the economy of Germany for more than a century, and some believe inflicted damage on the German psyche that would not be exorcised until the late twentieth century. It was 1618, as the Pilgrims hesitated about their future, that Protestant Bohemian hotheads threw the Hapsburg ambassadors out of a window in Prague's Hradcany castle; they were lucky to land on a dung heap. In November 1620, as *Mayflower* struggled towards Cape Cod, the Hapsburgs won the great battle of the White Mountain, just outside Prague, and took a terrible revenge on the Bohemian Protestant leadership. To us, these may seem obscure struggles in faraway countries of which we know little. Not to the Pilgrims. The Hapsburgs were the archenemies of Protestant religion, and their victory would mean a Calvary for Protestant Holland, where they lived. The Pilgrims' own fate could be all too easily imagined. The dangers from "wild men and wild animals" on a wild North American shore might look less terrible if the alternative was the treatment the Spanish Inquisition kept for obstinate heretics.

In the end, thanks to the feats of arms of great Protestant captains like the king of Sweden, Gustavus Adolphus, and to the rising power of Cardinal Richelieu's France, the war ended in defeat for Spain, in Spanish recognition of Dutch independence and the beginning of the Golden Age of Dutch trade, intellectual flowering, and art. But as the war clouds gathered, that was far from the likeliest outcome. "Great miseries," wrote Bradford, "might befall them in this place, for the twelve years of truce were now out and there was nothing but the beating of drums and preparing for war the events of which are always uncertain. The Spaniard might prove as cruel as the savages of America and the famine and pestilence as sore here as there."

Almost as an afterthought, Bradford added another reason for settling in America. "Lastly," he wrote, "and which was not least, a great hope and inward zeal they had of laying some good foundations, or at least to make some way thereunto, for the propagating and advancing the gospel of Christ in those remote parts of the world." Later settlers in New England, as we shall see, saw missionary work among the Native Americans as an important part of their reasons to cross the ocean. For the Pilgrims, it seems to have been one motive, but not the decisive one.

They were not alone at that time in thinking of moving to the New World. In the late 1620s, more aristocratic leaders of the Puritan party, led by the earl of Warwick, Lord Brooke, Lord Saye and Sele, his son Nathaniel Fiennes, and John Pym, one of the most powerful of the Puritan members of the House of Commons, thought seriously about emigrating to a new colony at several sites, including New Providence Island, off the coast of what is now Nicaragua. It was only after some years of hesitation that the members of that group changed their minds and decided to stay in England and fight it out with the king. Other Puritans, far more powerful and influential than the exiled Pilgrims in Holland, organized a mass migration of the godly to Massachusetts in 1630. Indeed there is a deep underlying irony to the story of the Pilgrims' emigration, in that little more than twenty years later their fellow Protestants won an English civil war and overthrew the Stuart dynasty that was persecuting them.

The practical question, for Brewster and Robinson and their congregation, was where to go. Some were attracted by reports of the fertility of what was then called Guiana, meaning the northern coast of South America. Others thought that was too near the Spanish colonies for safety, and wanted to be in an English jurisdiction. It was not as if they could choose among a wide variety of established English-speaking colonies in North America. They had read Thomas Hariot's account of the ill-fated colony planted by Walter Raleigh at Roanoke on the North Carolina outer banks, and descriptions of Guiana, by Raleigh himself and others. Everyone had read Richard Hakluyt's *Voyages* and its sequel, *Purchas his Pilgrims*. They were familiar with John Smith's glowing descriptions of Virginia. They had read also terrifying descriptions of the supposed cruelty of the Native Americans. William Bradford had heard that they flayed their prisoners alive with scallop shells and the like. Such things, Bradford wrote, "could not but move the very bowels of men to grate within them," though in all honesty they could hardly have been more cruel than contemporary Europeans; and indeed the Pilgrims were understandably nervous about settling too close to the "jealous Spaniard."[8]

They had been pressed to join in the Dutch scheme for settling at the mouth of the Hudson, but even if they feared the new Scots king on the English throne and rejected the official religion of England, they still saw themselves as English, not Dutch. There was only one existing English colony in America, and that was Virginia, the new and fragile settlement around Jamestown. After much debate, they decided to see if they would be allowed to settle there, or somewhere near. They set out to use such contacts as they had to see how the king in London and his government might respond if they decided to try to do so.

Brewster had first made inquiries when he was secretly in London. Obviously he was not the person to approach the king. Instead the Leiden church chose two of its deacons, both among the more prosperous of its members, John Carver and Robert Cushman, as emissaries to go to England and explore the government's mood. Carver came from Doncaster in south Yorkshire, not far up the Great North Road from Scrooby, but was not a member of the Scrooby congregation; he had made his way separately to Leiden and had married the sister of John Robinson's wife. Cushman, a wool comber from Canterbury, was not on good terms with Robinson, but was a trusted member of the Leiden congregation.

Because of Brewster's family history, the Pilgrim emissaries were not entirely without influential friends at court and in the Virginia Company, which was formed to promote colonization in North America. There were the Sandys brothers, sons of that Edwin Sandys who as archbishop of York[9] had been Brewster's father's employer. One, Sam, was the tenant of Scrooby manor and so Brewster's landlord. Another, the younger Sir Edwin Sandys, became treasurer of the Virginia Company. All were strong Puritans. A newer friend was Sir Robert Naunton, a friend of the younger Edwin Sandys, a man with Puritan sympathies who in 1618 became the king's principal secretary of state. The story goes that Sandys persuaded Naunton to approach King James and ask him whether these people could live with liberty of conscience in America with the king's gracious protection, and do their bit both to enlarge his dominions and to preach the gospel to the heathen. That was a good and honest notion, replied His Majesty, and how could they make a profit?

"Fishing," replied Sir Robert.

"So God have my soul," said James, "'tis an honest trade. 'Twas the Apostles' own calling."

James advised the would-be Pilgrims to consult the bishops. But they knew enough not to have anything to do with their persecutors. The conclusion they drew was that they should make the best of the vague approbation they seemed to have from the king, and to accept that he would not give them formal approval under his seal.

Besides the most favorable attitude they could procure from the king, in order to make their expedition a success, the Pilgrims needed two things. They would need some kind of title to the land they would settle on. And they would need capital, and quite a lot of it, for a ship or ships, and supplies for long enough to see their colony established, including food, drink, tools, weapons, seed, and trade goods to barter with the Indians.

At this time their courage was sorely tested by news of what had happened to another group of would-be emigrants. Some 180 members of Francis Johnson's Ancient Church in Amsterdam, under their Elder Francis Blackwell, a man Bradford accused of betraying members of his church, had sailed for Virginia. They were blown by northwesterly winds beyond their course and could not find the bay they were looking for. "Mr. Blackwell is dead, and Mr. Maggner the captain, yea, there are dead 130 persons . . . they were packed together like herrings. They had among them the flux [diarrhea] so as it is here rather wondered at that so many are alive than that so many are dead." Robert Cushman, who reported this to Leiden, added bravely that he saw "none here discouraged much but rather desire to learn to beware by other men's harms, and to amend that wherein they have failed."

Right at the beginning of their negotiations, in 1617, Brewster and Robinson sent a carefully worded paper to the Council for Virginia in London, presenting their religious views in the least threatening manner. The verbal skill with which they set about this would have done credit to their archenemies, the Jesuits. They acknowledged the Thirty-nine Articles, the official summary of the Church of England's beliefs, and said they wanted to remain in communion with it. They would be obedient to the king unless he commanded them to do things that were "against God's Word," and they gave an unenthusiastic acceptance to the authority of the bishops. No synod or other body they would set up could have ecclesiastical authority except with the king's authority, and they would "give unto all superiors due honour." These assurances— which, were they not from persons of such moral seriousness, would have to be called weasel words—were far from expressing the Pilgrims' real views on religious authority and church government. (They later explained their views rather more frankly in two letters to a certain Sir John Wolstenholme, one of the great London merchants of his day, who was a member of the Virginia Company. They told him that they agreed on most important questions with the French Reformed—that is, Calvinist— churches. They would willingly take the oath of supremacy to the king as head of the Church of England if the oath of allegiance was not considered enough.)

These assurances were enough to satisfy Sir Edwin Sandys and the gentlemen of his majesty's council for Virginia, or so Sandys wrote to Robinson and Brewster. They wrote back assuring Sandys of their commitment, pointing out, realistically, that "well weaned from the delicate milk of our mother country," they had little to lose, and were "knit together as a body in a most strict and sacred bond."

The authorities in London had long allowed groups of settlers to set up on large tracts of land what were called "particular plantations," which meant, roughly, private colonies.

In June 1619, the Virginia Company granted a "patent," or license, to set up a colony in North America to a certain John Wincop, who was a chaplain and tutor in the household of the Puritan Thomas Fiennes-Clinton, earl of Lincoln, who had recently died, and several members of whose family later emigrated to Massachusetts. Wincop was a sort of straw man. He was to hold the patent on behalf of the Leiden Pilgrims. Its terms have not survived. On February 2, 1620, another patent to settle in North America was granted by the Virginia Company to a certain John Peirce, an associate of Thomas Weston, and two further "Peirce patents" were granted later. Unfortunately the terms of those patents have not survived either. Historians argue about whether a patent could have been given by the Virginia Company for settlement as far north as the Hudson, which Bradford gives as the Pilgrims' destination. Probably they hoped to settle somewhere near the future site of New York, so as to be comfortably remote from royal authority in Jamestown, but hoped that a patent from the Virginia Company would be valid as far north as the Hudson. The Virginia Company's third charter, of 1612, had gifted it with land as far north and east as the middle of Long Island.

The long-established (London) Virginia company had succeeded in founding the settlement at Jamestown that is the origin of the present state of Virginia. In the course of 1620, however, another company, called the Plymouth Company, after its headquarters in the English city of Plymouth, was founded. Its members included a veteran adventurer in North America, Sir Ferdinando Gorges, and "sundry honorable lords." Their intention was to settle colonies to the north, from the region of Philadelphia up across Maine into Canada.

Given the approval, however vague or grudging, of the king's council and one or more patents from the Virginia Company, which offered a reasonable prospect of getting title to a sizeable tract of land beyond the sea, the next challenge was to find the capital to finance the venture. In the end Weston collected about seventy investors, mostly from London, who put in sums from five hundred pounds down. "Some were Gentlemen," wrote John Smith, of Virginia fame, "some merchants, some handycrafts men . . . they are not a corporation but knit together by voluntary combination with constraint or penalty, aiming to do good and plant religion." According to Smith, they put in a total of seven thousand pounds, a very substantial sum in the money of the time, the majority of which, as we shall see, never ended up supplying the colonists.[10] The motives of the backers were, as ever, mixed. Some, no doubt, were chiefly moved by the wish to "do good and plant religion." Others, Thomas Weston among them, were businessmen, primarily interested in profit.

An agreement was drawn up on July 1, 1620, between the business backers, called the Adventurers, and those who were planning to emigrate. The agreement created shares of ten pounds' face value each. Every Pilgrim would own one such share, and if he also put in ten pounds' worth in money or supplies, he would get two shares. Women and children over sixteen would each count for a share, and children between ten and sixteen would count for half a share. The Pilgrims and the adventurers together would create a "joint stock" and partnership for seven years, and all profits, whether from farming, fishing, or trading, would accrue to the joint stock. At the end of the seven years, the capital and the profits would be equally divided between the adventurers and the Pilgrims. Anyone who joined the colony or invested in it between the signing of the agreement and the end of the seven years would be given a share pro rata. In the meantime, until the end of the seven years, the settlers would have their food, drink, and clothing paid for out of the common stock.

From the start there was contention and dispute, then resentment, about this agreement, and in particular about the way Weston and some of the insiders among the adventurers altered the terms of deal. To be fair to Weston and his partners, he had never disguised his hope to make substantial profits.

Also at this stage, as the enterprise was moving forward to the Pilgrims' departure, a new element appeared for the first time. To the Leiden congregation or those among it who decided to make the journey, and the adventurers of various kinds who invested, there was now added a third group, the "strangers," people who for reasons of their own decided to join the migration, but who were not members of the Leiden congregation or even necessarily in agreement with its strong and godly motivation.

OVER THE CENTURIES, THE PILGRIMS AND THEIR DECISION to emigrate from Holland have taken their place in the great American national myth that is sometimes called American exceptionalism. It is seen as the beginning of a story that leads through the Revolution to the creation of American democracy. The *Mayflower* Compact—by which, for compelling reasons at the time, the Pilgrims bound themselves together before they landed on American soil—has been interpreted as a founding act of American liberty and constitutional government. Indeed, the Pilgrims have been endowed, in anachronistic retrospect, with a sense of universal mission.

This idea was given brilliant expression by the great scholar of New England culture, Perry Miller, in an essay called *Errand into the Wilderness*. Miller took his text and his title from a sermon delivered in 1670 by a certain Reverend Samuel Danforth. He called it *A Brief Recognition of New England's Errand into the Wilderness*. Miller makes a bold claim:

> The Bay Colony was not a battered remnant of suffering Separatists thrown up on a rocky shore; it was an organized task force of Christians, executing a flank attack on the corruptions of Christendom. These Puritans did not flee to America; they went to work out that complete reformation which was not yet accomplished in England and in Europe.[11]

It is important not to misstate Miller's thesis. For one thing, he was thinking primarily, not of William Brewster and the Plymouth settlers, but of John Winthrop and the far more ambitious migration to Massachusetts. Miller even goes out of his way to contrast the nobility of John Winthrop's vision of a "city set upon a hill" with the more humdrum aspirations of the Plymouth Pilgrims, who left Leiden simply to "get out while the going was good," though to do him justice he also praises the "great hymn" that William Bradford wrote about the Pilgrims' landfall in America as perhaps the very greatest passage in all New England's literature. For another, his concern is not so much with the glory of the Puritans' achievement, but with explaining the disappointment, the sense of "let-down," to be found in the "jeremiad" literature of the second and third generation in New England.

Overlooking the fierce disputes of historians of seventeenth-century New England theology—disputes almost as hot as those that divided English churchmen themselves in the seventeenth century—in the 1950s the United States, on the one hand, was able to exult in unprecedented military and economic power, and at the same time was locked into an ideological conflict with Soviet communism. Historians at the time, following the lead of Perry Miller and others, developed a universalist theory of the motives that brought the Puritans to New England. In this theory, English Puritans, impelled by a conviction that it was England's destiny to lead the world towards religious and political salvation, emigrated to North America with a clear intention of serving as an example to England, to Europe, and to the world, and so committed the United States that was to be born one hundred and fifty years later to a crusade for liberty and democracy.

By the 1970s, in a time when such ambitious definitions of the American historical mission were out of fashion, historians took another look at such interpretations.[12] They pointed out that 1950s historians had misunderstood or exaggerated the meaning of the most famous phrase in New England literature. This was the key sentence in John Winthrop's lay sermon, *A Model of Christian Charity*. As everyone knows, Winthrop said,

> Men shall say of succeeding plantacions: the lord make it like that of New England: for . . . we shall be as a Citty upon a Hill, the eies of all people are uppon us.

John Winthrop, a Puritan Suffolk squire, spoke these words on board the ship *Arbella*, before he had set foot in America, indeed before he had left England. He was not preaching any universal message of liberty or democracy. He was pointing out that, in the hard times that he expected lay ahead, people in other plantations, that is, in future colonies, would be judging how well the Puritans on their way to Massachusetts had followed the Christian injunction to charity. He never spoke of returning to England. He rarely if ever returned to this line of thought in his later, voluminous writings. There is no evidence whatever that Winthrop saw his future colony as a beacon to the world, or even that it would be morally exceptional. To the extent he and his friends were seeking liberty, it was not political freedom, but simply the freedom to practice the Protestant religion in the way they believed right, and in particular without the ceremonies that Puritans saw as a corrupt legacy of Roman Catholic practice.

In the same way, we should not attribute to the Pilgrims motives or beliefs that were far from their minds. They did not see themselves as forerunners or forefathers or founders of a republic still five generations in the future. The Pilgrims lived in their own time, children of that time, quite unaware of the vast superstructure of patriotism and ideology that would be balanced on their shoulders. As they got ready for their momentous and perilous voyage, they had enough to worry about in their own time. They set forth to escape the danger of persecution, and above all to keep together the congregation that, they profoundly believed, obeyed God's wish for them and their children.

CHAPTER FOUR

Voyage and Landfall

W HEN THE GREAT DAY CAME AT LAST, JOHN ROBINSON, too old (in his forties!) to make the journey himself[1] and unwilling to abandon the majority of his flock, preached on a text from the book of Ezra: "And there at the river, by Ahava, I proclaimed a fast, that we might humble ourselves before our God, and seek of him a right way for us, and for our children."[2]

So learned a student of the Bible would not have chosen the text for a sermon on an occasion of such emotional importance, for his congregation and for him, without care. It might be, and in fact it was, the last sermon he preached to his beloved flock. In the book of Ezra, from which he had chosen his text, the people of Israel are still captives in Babylon, but the Persian king of kings, Artaxerxes, is sympathetic.[3] An advance party has already left to set about the rebuilding of the Temple. Now Ezra has won the king's permission, and the main body of those Jewish exiles who want to leave Babylon is ready to begin a seven-hundred-mile trek across the desert to the Holy Land. So Ezra's fast is a symbol that the children of Israel, duly humbling themselves before God, are asking his blessing on their journey as they set forth to build a new

SHIPS IN HARBOR *(Dutch seascape)*
*(VerWer painting courtesy of the Pilgrim Hall Museum, Plymouth, MA,
reprinted with permission)*

Jerusalem. Equally, John Robinson is proposing, not thanksgiving, in the sense of a feast, but a fast. Such was the Puritan instinct.

On August 22, 1620, the Pilgrims[4] traveled from one of the Leiden canals twenty miles or so to Delfshaven on the broad Maas estuary,[5] where they embarked on a little sixty-ton ship they had bought, the *Speedwell*.[6] Robinson, their beloved pastor, came with them, and a crowd of Dutch people gathered to watch them set forth on their fateful voyage. By chance, a picture that was almost certainly drawn by an eyewitness has survived.[7] Heavy-laden boats, watched by indifferent ducks, carry passengers out to the *Speedwell*, with the towers of Rotterdam faintly visible in the mist in the background. The Pilgrims must have asked themselves whether their God would look kindly on their adventure. It is a great mistake to think of seventeenth-century Puritans as cold, undemonstrative people. The parting was emotional, with sighs and sobs and prayers and tears. "Their reverend pastor falling down on his knees (and they all with him) with watery cheeks commended them with fervent prayers to the Lord and His blessing."[8]

There were perhaps fifty-seven men, women, and children from the Leiden church who sailed "with a prosperous wind" to Southampton in the center of the southern English Channel coast.[9] It was there that the Leiden Pilgrims met with three other groups of people who would share their enterprise. There were those who had come from London and elsewhere in England to settle with them, named the "strangers" by William Bradford. There were about forty-eight of them.[10] Some shared the Leiden Pilgrims' religious commitments; others did not. Some were simply young Londoners who hoped to prosper and in particular become landowners in America, a prohibitively expensive ambition for them in settled, still partly feudal England.[11] Some eighteen of them were "indentured servants," young people, that is, who agreed to work for low wages, or no wages at all, for seven years in return for their keep and for freedom to start a new life in America after their years of servitude were over.

The leader of the strangers was Christopher Martin, from Billericay in Essex. He was a religious migrant: He had twice been in trouble with the bishop's court for rejecting the Anglican doctrine on baptism and the sacraments. Another notable stranger was Myles Standish, a professional soldier, veteran of the Low Country wars, who had been hired as the Pilgrims' military commander. He came from Lancashire, traditionally a Catholic county, and was born in the Isle of Man. Small of stature—he was known as "Captain Shrimp"—he had red hair and a dangerous temper. He thought nothing of cutting off an Indian's head if he thought it was the right thing to do. But he was a brave and committed member of the party, and the Pilgrims were to owe him a lot for his military knowledge and his courage before their adventures were over.

There were the sailors, two dozen or so altogether, including experienced seamen and agile young monkeys to scamper up and down the rigging. The Master and one-quarter owner, Christopher Jones, came from Essex, staunch Protestant territory, but had bought a house at Rotherhithe on the south bank of the Thames a mile or so downstream from London Bridge. Two of the four mates, John Clark and Robert Coppin,[12] had both been to North America before. The crew also included a ship's doctor, Giles Heale, over and above the Pilgrims' own physician from Leiden, Samuel Fuller; a master gunner and his mate; a cooper, or barrel-maker, John Alden, hired in Southampton; and a ship's carpenter, skilled enough to repair a main deck beam while *Mayflower* was in the mid-Atlantic. Then there were the Adventurers, the business people Weston had rounded up to invest in the project. Few of them actually traveled to America. But their influence, and their demands, were to be felt constantly for the first ten years of the colony's existence.

Weston had agreed to supply the expedition with a ship and capital on certain conditions. The ship he had chartered was the *Mayflower*, of 180 tons' "burthen," meaning she could carry 180 tons of cargo. She was about one hundred feet long overall and, because both bows and stern were steeply raked, less at the waterline. Not big by modern standards, but bigger than many a ship that made some of the most memorable voyages of exploration. (Drake's *Golden Hind*, earlier called the *Pelican*, which circumnavigated the world in three years, capturing some large Spanish treasure ships on the way, was only of 120 tons' burthen.) *Mayflower* had three decks, a deep waist, and six sails on three masts: square-rigged "courses" (mainsails) and topsails on the fore and main masts, a spritsail on the bowsprit sticking out at the front, and a lateen (fore-and-aft) sail on the mizzen or rear mast. She carried two boats, a long boat and the "shallop," a sort of twenty-one-foot dinghy. ("Shallop" was the English version of the French *chaloupe*, itself derived from the Dutch word *sloep*, which also gives us the English word "sloop."[13]) *Mayflower* was at least twelve years old and had been employed in the wine trade from Bordeaux to London. As a consequence the ullage from the wine casks had spilled into the bilges, acting as an antiseptic in the filth left there, so that she was a "sweet," meaning a healthy, ship. The Pilgrims were not troubled with illness, even though they were crammed together below decks in unsanitary conditions.

The North Atlantic and even more the American coast were dangerous places in those days, full of pirates, privateers, and freebooters. The Pilgrims anticipated having to defend themselves against Spaniards, Frenchmen, or the Dutch, as well as Native Americans. So *Mayflower* carried twelve artillery pieces, eight "minions" and four "sakers."[14]

Thomas Weston had come down from London bringing money to stock up with supplies, which was welcome, but also bringing a revised version of the contract for the Pilgrims to sign, which they refused to do. Weston, Cushman, and Carver had agreed the changes, but the Leiden leaders had not seen them, and they were annoyed. Robinson, in particular, wrote from Leiden with unconcealed irritation. Weston wanted to omit two clauses. One provided that the settlers' houses, gardens, and improved land should not be counted as part of the common stock to be divided, but should remain the property of the settlers. The second clause Weston wanted to strike out allowed the settlers "two days a week for their own private employment."

It has been argued that the prospect that Parliament would agree to a fishing monopoly would affect the profitability of the venture, so that Weston's proposed changes were justified. But this was only one example of Weston's constant attempts to screw more money out of those who were, after all, taking the main risks. He came down from London to try to get the "planters" to sign the new version of the agreement. They refused. Weston was "much offended and told them they must look to stand on their own legs." They sailed on to Plymouth, some 200 miles further west, leaving their principal investor much disgruntled.

It was not as simple as that, because the Pilgrims still owed nearly one hundred pounds, a large sum, for supplies, and Weston would not hand over a single penny more. They cleared two-thirds of the debt or so in the end by selling whatever they could spare. This included oil (needed for cooking and light), some armor and weapons, and a very large amount—something between three and four thousand pounds weight—of butter, which they had overprovided.[15] They were left without soles for some of their shoes and swords for some belts, but at least they had paid off some sixty pounds of their debt. However, this was the first of a long series of disagreements between the Pilgrims and their financial backers, the Adventurers, and in particular with the Adventurers' leader, Weston.

Mayflower's voyage was, on the part of the Adventurers, a hardheaded commercial investment, and one which they, and in particular Weston, took advantage of to bilk the religious Pilgrims of large amounts of money, in part with the cooperation of an unscrupulous member of the Pilgrims' own inner circle.

The Plymouth Company petitioned for a fishing monopoly. The dispute over fishing rights was not resolved, and the Plymouth Company's venture did not "pass the seals" (that is, did not become law) until after the Pilgrims had set sail. Faced with at best uncertainty about fishing rights, and the possible loss of profit from fishing, it was understandable that a shrewd businessman like Weston should seek to renegotiate the deal. However, it appears that Weston, having raised seven thousand pounds from his investors, laid out not much more than fifteen hundred pounds in equipping the settlers.

The adventurers' desire for a commercial return was entirely understandable. They were being asked to make a substantial investment: a ship, sails, armaments, food, drink, supplies not only for the voyage but at least until the colony could feed itself, tools of all kinds, and trade goods to exchange for whatever the native Americans could supply, which essentially meant beaver and other furs.

We do not know exactly what stores *Mayflower* carried, but a list of what a similar ship, *Talbot*—with a similar number of passengers and crew—took to Massachusetts nine years later gives a rough idea of the large quantities that would have been needed. *Talbot* carried:

1. 45 tuns of beer
2. 16 tuns of Malaga and Canary wine
3. 6 tuns of water
4. 12,000 pounds of bread
5. 22 hogsheads of beef
6. 40 bushels of peas
7. 20 bushels of oatmeal
8. 1,400 pounds of saltfish
9. 96 pounds of candle
10. 2 terces [small barrels] of malt vinegar
11. 1½ bushels of mustard seed
12. 20 gallons of olive oil, from Gallipoli or Majorca
13. 2 firkins of soap
14. 20 gallons of Spanish wine
15. 4,000 billets of firewood
16. 10 firkins of butter
17. 1,000 pounds of cheese
18. 20 gallons of hard liquor ["Aquavit"][16]

Fifty years earlier, Martin Frobisher's expedition set forth with a crew of thirty-five on what might be a long voyage in search of a northeast passage to China to the north of the Russian land mass.

He loaded his ship *Gabriel* with enough beef and bacon for four days a week and salt cod for the other three days (and he expected to be away for many months), together with 40 bushels of peas, 36 bushels of flour, and 76 hundredweight of hard ship's biscuit, as well as more than 3,000 gallons of beer and £100 worth of fine French wine. Sixteenth-century English sailors ate and drank well, because they had to. It has been calculated that they consumed between 5,500 and 7,000 calories a day, about twice what a healthy American eats today.[17] Hard physical work in bitterly cold weather, including climbing the rigging several times a day, hauling heavy sails up the mast with the capstan, and raising a massive iron anchor with the windlass, demanded plenty of fuel for human muscles. The massive provisioning of ships like *Mayflower* reminds us of the sheer human effort that went into the voyages of exploration and settlement.

Thanks to the magic mechanics of block and tackle, these bulky stores, or something like them, were hoisted aboard *Mayflower*. She would also have carried tools, weapons, including heavy cannon, shot and powder, and some live animals, certainly dogs, probably sheep, goats, and poultry, as well as one hundred passengers and twenty to thirty crew. Horses and cattle came later.

The original plan was to take two ships. The smaller, *Speedwell*, which they had brought from Delfshaven, would stay in America for coasting and trading voyages, but *Mayflower* would return to England. They had not gone very far west from Southampton, however, when *Speedwell*, with about thirty souls on board, began to ship water. Bradford called it "as leaky as a sieve." They put in to the beautiful estuary of the Dart and tied up at Dartmouth, where the leaks were caulked, and set out again. But when they had gone some three hundred miles beyond Land's End, the westernmost cape of English soil, *Speedwell* began to leak again, and they had to turn back and put into Plymouth. It turned out that the leaks were deliberate. *Speedwell*'s master had intentionally overmasted her and

MAYFLOWER AT SEA
*(Photo courtesy of Plimoth Plantation, Inc., www.plimoth.org,
reprinted with permission)*

crowded on too much sail.[18] He was afraid the expedition would run out of food, and that *Mayflower* would make sure it kept all the supplies. So he hit on this "stratagem," as Bradford called it, to get out of his agreement. In the end the leaders agreed to cram *Speedwell*'s passengers into *Mayflower*, which was all the easier because a number of them, including Robert Cushman, who had been the Pilgrims' trusted agent until the row with Weston, gave up and decided to stay at home.

Weeks had been wasted in wrangling with Weston at Southampton and in turning back into first Dartmouth and then Plymouth, so it was September 6 before *Mayflower* sailed on alone, with exactly one hundred passengers. That was perilously late to cross the North Atlantic in a ship of that age. For a few days the weather was fine and the sailing pleasant. But then *Mayflower* was caught and savagely shaken in the equinoctial gales. The ship became leaky above the waterline, and one of the main beams supporting the deck began to be bowed. But by good fortune they had brought a big screw with them from Holland, possibly the screw from the Brewster's print shop, which they were able to use to support the deck while they reinforced it with a new post.[19] The sailors wanted to earn their wages, but they were understandably "loath to hazard their lives too desperately." Jones and his men stuck to their duty, though, and Brewster and his company "committed themselves to the will of God, and resolved to proceed."

It was no easy decision. It was not that sailing to America was such a very unheard-of affair. Literally hundreds of European ships, some of them far smaller than *Mayflower*, had been crossing the Atlantic every year for more than a century, since Cabot had first made landfall at the northernmost tip of Newfoundland in 1497. By 1620, thousands of European sailors were accustomed to spending the summers fishing on the Grand Banks and along the shores of Newfoundland, Nova Scotia, and Maine. Along the quayside in Bristol, or for that matter in La Rochelle in France or Porto in Portugal, you could find dozens of men any day who had sailed to America, and were only too happy to tell you about the wonderful catches they had made, and the strange and alarming ways of the Indians.

The great majority of them, however, had taken good care to sail in the summertime. *Mayflower* was on the North Atlantic, hundreds of miles from land or any hope of rescue, at the height of the fierce autumn storms. Bradford reports that the wind was often so strong and the seas so high that for days on end they lay "at hull," the contemporary sailors' way of saying that they reefed the sails as short as they could and drifted with the winds. Conditions on board in the crowded, airless space between decks, pitching and tossing in the great Atlantic waves, can only be imagined. The Master's cabin was spacious, and so too were the cabins for the fortunate few who could afford to pay for them. But for the crew and most of the passengers it was stuffy and no doubt smelly, too.

While they were at sea one child was born, to Elizabeth, the wife of Stephen Hopkins, and most appropriately named Oceanus. One of the sailors died. He was, says Bradford, a "proud and very profane young man," with the unpleasant habit of cursing those passengers who were suffering from seasickness. "It pleased God . . . to smite him with a grievous disease, of which he died in a desperate manner."[20] Another young man, John Howland, later one of the leading members of the colony, would have been swept overboard, but he managed to catch hold of the topsail halyards and held on even when he was many fathoms under water, until he could be pulled up and rescued with a boathook. The only passenger who did die was a certain William Butten or Button, a servant to the Pilgrims' doctor, Samuel Fuller. Ninety-nine in all would complete the crossing.

WHILE THE PASSENGERS WHILED AWAY THE TIME AS BEST they could, below decks as long as the weather was rough, reading by candlelight or playing cards and games like Nine Men's Morris (the little board version of the outdoor game Shakespeare mentions as "filled up with mud" in *A Midsummer Night's Dream*), on deck, Captain Christopher Jones and his mates were navigating *Mayflower* towards her destiny.

They were only able to cross the ocean at all because of the huge improvements that had been made over the past century in the art and the technology of navigation. It was this nautical revolution that made possible the great voyages of discovery, down the coast of Africa, eastward to India and the Spice Islands, and westward across the Atlantic, and the more humdrum expansion of Europe overseas through fishing and trade. It was the work of Spanish, Portuguese, Italian, Basque, French, and Breton as well as English seamen, and of collaboration between learned men, puzzling out the theory in their studies, and rugged, often illiterate mariners, reporting what happened on the high seas. It was sea captains, to take just one example, who reported that magnetic north varied by as much as 22 percent from one location to another.

Navigation relies on pinpointing a ship's position by latitude and longitude. Until the accurate modern chronometer was invented by John Harrison in the early eighteenth century, latitude was far easier to compute than longitude.[21] Although they could compute latitude, the seamen of early modern Europe relied for the most part on what is called "dead reckoning," short for "deduced reckoning." They had four devices to help them, all of which had been decisively improved in the hundred years or so before the Pilgrims made their voyage. They needed to know the direction of their course, their speed, and the time they had been traveling. They charted their course with a compass. In the Middle Ages this was a floating magnetized needle, but by the sixteenth century it was mounted on a gimbal so that it was not affected by the movement of the ship. They measured their speed with the log and line. This was a "chip log," or board, attached to a line, which was tossed over the stern. The line was marked with a knot at intervals of a nautical mile, which is why nautical miles, to this day, are called "knots." Time was measured, not with clocks, but with hour glasses. These were figure-eight-shaped glass vessels. Sand trickled steadily through a small aperture from the upper vessel to the lower, so that they had to be reversed at regular intervals, usually every four hours. When the hour glass had emptied the top vessel, a sailor would strike a bell, and another sailor would count how many knots of line had run out, which again is why ship's watches, mostly four hours long to this day, are still measured in bells.

Captain Jones could also calculate his latitude by using one of a series of instruments that had also been improved over the past century from their medieval originals. Each of these—the astrolabe, the quadrant, and the cross-staff—enabled the navigator to calculate latitude by measuring the height of a celestial body. He could do this in day time by pointing his instrument at the sun, protecting his eyes with smoked glass, and at night by observing the pole star, or North Star, in Latin *Polaris*. The cross-staff, the simplest, most robust instrument, was a rod, square in section, with a cross-piece that could be made to slide up and down. The seaman fixed the end of the staff to the bone under his eye, and moved the cross-piece until the bottom rested on the horizon, and the top on the star. He then looked up his latitude in printed tables that were already available by the time of *Mayflower*'s voyage.

The early seventeenth-century navigator, who was often illiterate, could use one further piece of equipment, the traverse-board, which enabled him to chart the direction of his course by sticking pegs into a board. In the Mediterranean, since time immemorial, sailors had plotted their course in terms of eight winds corresponding to eight points of the compass, as we call them. In the early sixteenth century, Breton seamen replaced the eight winds with thirty-two points of the compass "rose," and began to produce navigational tables. Even earlier, sailors began to produce what were called *routiers,* or charts of the coasts sailors followed, soon corrupted in English into "rutters." (Some scholars believe that Homer's *Odyssey* grew out of ancient Greek sailors' route books for the Mediterranean, more than two thousand years earlier.[22])

Among the oldest known rutters is that of a French Basque, Pierre Garcie, for the Atlantic coast of Europe from the Straits of Gibraltar to Britain. This was written as early as the 1480s and published shortly after 1500. By 1579, transatlantic voyages were sufficiently common that Martin Hoyarsabal, another Basque, this time from Spain, published a guide to the Atlantic coast of what is now Canada. His work must be based on voyages of the 1560s and 1570s, for his *Voyages Avantureux* was published in French translation in 1579.[23]

Primitive as the tools available to him may seem to us, Captain Jones, with the help of his two experienced mates, succeeded in sailing his ship to within about one degree of latitude of his goal. There has been much argument about where he was, in fact, headed. It is fairly certain that, as Bradford directly stated years later,[24] they were bound for the present site of New York, the mouth of the Hudson River. The Dutch had discovered and were beginning to settle the Hudson River valley, and we have seen that if the Pilgrims had been willing to go there, the Dutch would have encouraged them and even given them some cattle to help. But the legendary deal, when the Dutch bought Manhattan from the Indians for twenty-four dollars, was still six years in the future. It seems as clear as can be that the expedition was indeed intended to settle at the mouth of the Hudson. The leaders must have interpreted their patent to mean that the present site of New York fell within the jurisdiction of Virginia, as, arguably, it did.

So when *Mayflower* made its landfall at eight in the morning of November 9—after two months and three days at sea—roughly halfway along the ocean side of Cape Cod, off a shore that reminded its passengers of the long sand beaches, backed with dunes, that run the length of the North Sea coast of Holland, Captain Jones turned south to follow the shore. At first, both the wind and the weather were fair. About three in the afternoon, however, after half a day's sailing, they found themselves among dangerous shoals and roaring breakers. From the "elbow" of the Cape, the island called Monomoy extends southward for several miles to Monomoy Point, then gives way to sandbanks. At right angles to Monomoy, another bar of sandbanks sticks out eastward into the ocean for five or six miles. This is Pollock Rip. The situation there looked so perilous that after some debate the master turned tail and sailed back northward again. For many years the canard has surfaced from time to time that Captain Jones had been bribed by the Dutch not to take his passengers to settle in the neighborhood they claimed. There is no serious reason to believe this. And besides, writes Admiral Samuel Eliot Morison with the voice of experience, "No seaman who has weathered Cape Cod needs any better explanation than a headwind on unbuoyed Pollock Rip to explain why *Mayflower* turned back." They turned back northward, and soon rounded the tip of Cape Cod.

The next morning they found themselves safe, for a moment at least. Provincetown Bay was so shallow that they had to wade in near-freezing weather "two bowshots," several hundred yards, with the result that many of them developed colds and coughs.

Before they landed, however, they took a precaution against another danger whose meaning has subsequently been much misunderstood. "Some," wrote the author of the relevant passage in

Mourt's Relation,[25] "[were] not well affected to unity and concord, but gave appearance of faction." The leaders, in other words, saw the advance warning signs of a mutiny, presumably among the strangers from London, rather than among the Leiden Pilgrims. So they insisted that all the adult males, including some of the servants, sign a paper agreeing "that we should combine together in one body, and to submit to such governors and government as we should agree to make and choose."

The text to which they set their hands read:

In the name of God, Amen. We whose names are underwritten, the loyal subjects of our dread sovereign lord King James, by the grace of God, of Great Britain, France and Ireland King, Defender of the Faith etc.

Having undertaken, for the glory of God, and advancement of the Christian faith, and honor of our king and country, a voyage to plant the first colony in the northern parts of Virginia, do by these presents solemnly and mutually in the presence of God and one of another, covenant and combine ourselves together into a civil body politic, for our better ordering and preservation, and furtherance of the ends aforesaid; and by virtue hereof to enact, constitute and frame such just and equal laws, ordinances, acts, constitutions, offices from time to time, as shall be thought most meet and convenient for the general good of the colony: unto which we promise all due submission and obedience.

This text, known as the Mayflower Compact, has been extravagantly hailed as one of the founding texts of American democracy. John Quincy Adams, for example, called it "perhaps the only instance in human history of that positive social compact that speculative philosophers have imagined as the only legitimate source of government."

This, with all due respect to the sixth president and to others who have seen the compact as a forerunner of the Declaration of Independence, is anachronistic, unhistorical nonsense. The compact was not a state paper. It was written, hurriedly, and signed almost a century and a half before the American Revolution. It cannot have been written as a founding document for an American nation, because there was at the time no such nation, nor any intention or even any conception of creating one. The Mayflower Compact goes out of its way to express formal loyalty to the king of England, though of course in crossing the Atlantic the leaders of the exploration wanted to put space between them and the Anglican bishops' observation of their religious practices. It was a document intended to bind together a group of Englishmen who were embarked on a potentially perilous venture, and specifically to unite those whose motives were essentially spiritual with those who had more worldly ambitions.

There was a second reason, beyond the fear of faction, that made the leaders seek collective commitment. By turning back from the breakers on Pollock Rip, they might be exceeding their formal authority to settle. Their authorization came from the Virginia Company, and while the mouth of the Hudson might be said to lie within the territory granted to the Virginia Company, Cape Cod was manifestly not. The law governing plantations was not firmly settled. But by landing and preparing to settle in *terra nullius*, no man's land, the Pilgrims might be breaking the law of England and—under the early Stuarts, much the same thing—they might be incurring the wrath of their "dread sovereign lord King James."

The compact, then, was not a groundbreaking statement of revolutionary democratic principles. It was a practical document to give the Pilgrim leaders cover, both with their followers and, if there should be any later comeback on their settlement outside the territory of the Virginia Company, with the English government.

It was also strongly influenced by the compacts and covenants with which separatist and other dissenting churches, including the church of Scrooby, bound their members to loyalty.

It was, finally, a practical device, a safeguard negotiated by leaders afraid of the possibility of a mutiny or disobedience that they could not suppress, and seeking—by making everyone sign it—to procure loyalty and hopefully make it harder for any such movement to recruit support. However justified or otherwise the leaders were in asking virtually all the adult male passengers to sign it, the danger of mutiny passed. Other, more immediate dangers demanded attention, and other questions had to be answered: Where were the Pilgrims to settle? How would they feed, shelter, and protect themselves? Would they survive?

CHAPTER FIVE

A Place of Habitation

B EING THUS PASSED THE VAST OCEAN, AND A SEA OF TROUBLES before in their preparation, they had no friends to welcome them nor inns to entertain or refresh their weather-beaten bodies, no houses or much less towns to repair to, to seek for succour." With those words, years later, William Bradford took stock of the situation that had faced him and his companions as they fell upon their knees at Provincetown and blessed the God of Heaven for delivering them from the "vast and furious ocean," and its "cruel and fierce storms." But their new condition, as he recalled it, was scarcely a great improvement over the perils and miseries of the voyage.

There was no Mount Pisgah, he said, from which they could look down on "a more goodly country to feed their hopes." Bradford moved from the Old Testament to the New: where the Apostle Paul had been shown kindness by the barbarians when he was rescued from shipwreck, the Pilgrims had no reason, from all they had heard, to expect much hospitality from the Indians. It was winter, and all they could see was "a hideous and desolate wilderness, full of wild beasts and wild men."

Bradford himself faced an immediate, personal catastrophe. His wife, Dorothy, was to drown at Provincetown. He recorded the bare fact laconically: "William Bradford his wife died soon after their arrival, and he married again and hath four children, three whereof are married."[1] Cotton Mather, in his history of New England, published more than eighty years later, adds something: "At their first landing, his dearest consort accidentally falling overboard, was drowned in the harbour."[2]

It has been suggested[3] that Dorothy Bradford's death was suicide, perhaps brought on by the very desolation of the prospect to which her husband had brought her, or even in some accounts by her remorse at having had an affair, either with Captain Jones of the *Mayflower* or with some other passenger. There is absolutely no evidence for these fantasies. They come from an article in a women's magazine, as far back as 1869, published as if they were true and based on family traditions, but which the author subsequently admitted she had made up.[4]

Other trials lay in wait for the Pilgrims. What could sustain them, Bradford reflected, but the Spirit of God and his Grace? He was comforted by the thought that their children would rightly say, "Our fathers were Englishmen which came over this great ocean, and were ready to perish in this wilderness; but they cried unto the Lord, and He heard their voice and looked on their adversity. Let them therefore praise the Lord, because He is good, and His mercies endure forever." There, before any material blessings had been vouchsafed, was the authentic spirit of thanksgiving.

There was no time to be lost, if they were to build shelter for themselves before the New England winter closed in. So that very first day, while the carpenter started to refit the shallop, which had been used as sleeping quarters on the voyage, and the children stretched their legs, and everyone marveled at the whales playing and spouting out in the Bay, and at the abundance of fish, mussels, and seabirds, a party of the stouter settlers set forth, heavily armed, to look for firewood and to reconnoiter Cape Cod. They came back having seen plenty of sassafras, highly prized at the time for its supposed medicinal value (it was thought to be a cure for syphilis), and with plenty of juniper as firewood, which smelled sweet when it burned. They had not seen any "wild men."

That did not mean that the Nausets of Cape Cod, who had had unpleasant experiences of how Europeans could behave, had not seen them. (The Cape Cod Indians had had a recent encounter with the English adventurer, Captain Thomas Hunt, who had kidnapped twenty Wampanoags and seven Nausets, enslaved them, and sold them in the slave market in Malaga, in southern Spain, of all places. By an amazing sequence of chances, the Pilgrims were to meet one of those enslaved Indians again.) The Nausets were keeping them under close, though discreet, surveillance.

The next day was the Sabbath, which, despite the urgent need to establish their settlement, was observed in their usual way. On Monday sixteen Pilgrims, led by Captain Standish, and including William Bradford and Stephen Hopkins, armed to the teeth, set forth again. Each man wore a corselet of steel body armor and carried a sword and a musket. They lumbered heavily off in single file to explore further down the peninsula. They had gone no more than a mile when they saw half a dozen Indians coming towards them with a dog. When they saw the Englishmen, the Indians sprinted into the woods, and though the Pilgrims followed their tracks for ten miles, they had no chance, encumbered as they were, of catching them. Nervously, they set sentries, pitched camp, lit fires, and settled down for the night.

In the morning they followed the tracks again, but without catching sight of the Indians, who were scouts themselves sent out to take a look at these new Englishmen.

Standish and his men now saw their first North American deer, but they were thirsty, so they were more delighted when they came upon a spring, now no more than a boggy patch, near what today is the car park and lookout point at Pilgrim Heights. They "sat us down and drank our first New England water with as much delight as ever we drunk drink before."[5] Seventeenth-century English folk were not used to drinking water, which was rightly thought unsafe; if they could not afford wine, they usually drank "small beer," a low-alcohol brew that was given even to children.

On they went, everywhere seeing signs of Indians, but nowhere seeing Indians themselves. They found what turned out to be Indian graves, and dug up a bow and some old rotten arrows, but put them back "because we thought it would be odious unto them to ransack their sepulchres." In this account written almost four hundred years ago, the excitement of this exploration, under the eyes of unseen men who might turn out to be dangerous and cruel enemies, is almost palpable. They pressed on, and found new stubble, from which corn had been harvested that very year, then strawberry patches, and an old iron ship's kettle; they thought it must have been left there by some of the many Europeans from the fisheries to the north who had passed that way. Then they found heaps of sand, which, when they excavated them with their swords, turned out to be baskets full of ample stores of Indian corn. There was far too much for them to carry, weighed down as they were with their armor, so they took some of the baskets, and carted off the loose corn in the ship's kettle, slung on a pole and carried between two men, and left what they could not take away to be picked up later. They were not stealing, as they saw it: they decided to come back and pay the Indians for as much more as they would give them later. To their surprise, they saw two Indian canoes. That night it rained heavily. They built a big fire and took turns standing sentry for as long as it took for six inches of musket match to burn.

In the morning they got lost in the woods, and found an Indian deer trap, "a very pretty device," thought Winslow, as artful as any

English rope maker could have made, made by bending a sapling as a spring, and scattering acorns to tempt the deer. William Bradford came up to look. The trap gave a sudden jerk, and he was caught by the leg. After they had got out of the wood, and seen three more deer and great flocks of wild geese and ducks, they fired a shot and the longboat (the shallop was still being mended) came to pick them up and take them back to *Mayflower* in Provincetown Harbor.

When the shallop was fixed at last they made another reconnaissance. By now it was freezing and six inches of snow lay on the ground. They were frightened of running into Indians. When they saw an Indian deer trap, they thought it was the entrance to an Indian village, so they all lit the wicks of their matchlock muskets. What they did find was the grave containing the skull of a man with long yellow hair. They argued whether it was a European who had died a natural death when living with the Indians, or one whom the Indians had killed and buried. (A surprising number of fishermen and explorers from half a dozen European countries were to be found on the North American coast by the early years of the seventeenth century.) Two sailors stumbled upon an Indian camp, empty, but with bowls, tray, and dishes, and venison stuffed into a hollow tree. That might be full of anthropological interest, but for the vulnerable Pilgrims it was frustrating and must have intensified their eerie feeling of being kept under observation by unseen watchers, all the more so when they saw the smoke of Indian campfires four or five miles off.

A third expedition went out a few days later. The Pilgrims had still not found a site with everything they needed: fertile land, fresh water in adequate quantity, and a good harbor. This time they went eighteen strong: seven Separatists, three from London, two from Leiden, two of the ship's mates, the gunner, and three of their sailors. The expedition returned to find that Susanna White had borne a son, whom she called Peregrine, after the Latin, *peregrinus*, for a wanderer or pilgrim. Less auspiciously, Francis Billington, son of the most troublesome family in the entire expedition,[6] nearly succeeded in blowing *Mayflower* up by firing off a fowling piece close to a half full barrel of gunpowder. By God's mercy, Winslow recorded, no harm was done.

The third reconnaissance party went some twenty miles south in the shallop, in bitter weather that froze their clothes and made them feel like coats of iron. They saw a dozen Indians on a beach on the bay side, busy with something black, but it was getting dark, and time to make camp. It wasn't until the morning that they realized that the black object was a grampus,[7] a small whale, five or six yards long, one of three that had been cast up on the beach. After a day of wandering they found a more elaborate grave site in a palisade, and Indian houses. They had settled down in camp for the night when, about midnight, they heard a "great and hideous cry." The sentries shouted "Arm! Arm!" so the Pilgrims got up and fired off a couple of muskets, and the noise stopped. Someone said it was wolves, recognizing the noise from an earlier voyage to Newfoundland.

They were having breakfast the next morning when they heard the same noise again. It was not wolves. Someone shouted, "They are men! Indians! Indians!" and before he had finished, arrows were zinging in on them. Captain Standish had a "snapchance" fowling piece, lighter and quicker to load than the five-foot-long muzzle-loading muskets, and he got off a shot. A brave Indian stood behind a tree, firing off his arrows. Three times muskets were fired at him, and still he stood there. Finally Standish put a shot close to his head, and away he went screaming horribly.

The Pilgrims thanked God that He had vanquished their enemies, and congratulated themselves that no one had been hurt, even though some coats that were hanging on the barricade they had put up the night before round the camp had been shot full of holes. Ever afterwards this skirmish was known as the "first

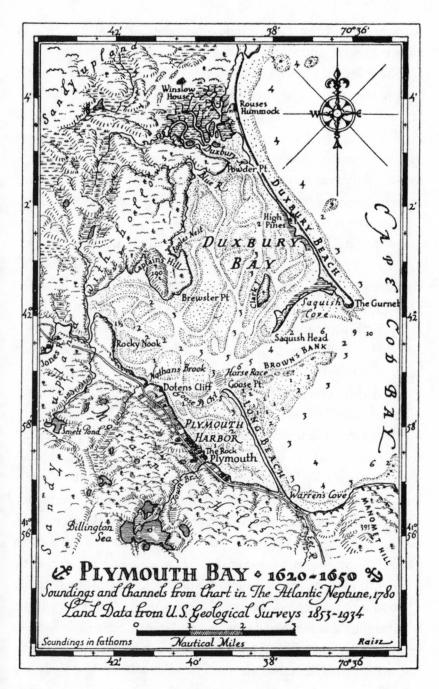

PLYMOUTH BAY COLONY
(Photo courtesy of Random House, Inc.)

encounter," and the place where it happened, in Eastham, is still known as First Encounter Beach.

The Pilgrims were no nearer to finding the secure and defensible site they needed for their plantation, and the weather was getting worse by the day. They had been debating whether to stay at Providence, or to sail to a place the Indians called Angawam, now Ipswich, Massachusetts, or to explore Patuxet, which is now Plymouth. Provincetown had much to recommend it, but they were not sure that the water supply would be adequate in summertime. Angawam was too far away.

So they decided to explore Plymouth, which had been mapped by Champlain, favorably described by Captain John Smith, and visited by several Europeans, most recently by Captain Thomas Dermer. Dermer had been employed by the great colonial adventurer, Sir Ferdinando Gorges, to explore the New England coast, and had actually been at Plymouth in June 1619, just over a year before the Pilgrims arrived there.

To decide whether or not they should settle at Plymouth, the Pilgrims sailed along the coast inside Cape Cod Bay, first south, then west towards the mainland. Their arrival was not auspicious. By the middle of the afternoon the weather had worsened, with rain, then snow, and rough seas, and so much wind that the shallop's mast was broken into three pieces and the sail fell overboard. The rudder was broken, too, and it was as much as two men could do to steer the boat with their oars. Coppin, one of *Mayflower*'s mates, who was in command of the shallop, missed the entrance to Plymouth Harbor, which is almost landlocked. A craft making for Plymouth from the open waters of Cape Cod Bay has to twist and turn through a chicane of dangerous sandbanks. Six miles of sandy beach stretch south from Duxbury like a breakwater to a headland called the Gurnet, before turning inland to a second point called Saquish. Closer to the shore, a spit of sand called the town beach, more than two miles long, reaches northwards from a point a couple of miles south of the site of the town, guarded on the seaward side by the Brown's Bank shallows.

Scholars argue about which headland Coppin mistook for which other one, and whether it was on Brown's Bank or on Saquish they were nearly wrecked. The long and short of it was that the shallop was heading for disaster when one of the steersmen, "a lusty man," took command, and urged on the rowers to greater efforts, so that they squeaked past Saquish head and into calmer water.

So the Pilgrim vanguard arrived in Plymouth, not—as in the nineteenth-century patriotic prints—with fife and drum, watched by cowering Indians, but staggering ashore, exhausted, drenched, and chilled to the bone. But at least they ended up safe on what came to be called, after a later Yankee farmer, Clark's Island in Plymouth Bay, five miles or so across the water from the site of the town. It was Friday night. They were so exhausted that they did not stir on Saturday, and on Sunday again they prayed and listened to the word of God. It was not until Monday that they were rested enough to sail across the sheltered waters of the bay to the foot of the Town Brook, and it was there that they began to build their settlement.

Of all the patriotic myth that has become encrusted on the genuine heroism of these brave and godly men, the cult of Plymouth Rock is the most implausible. There it stands, under a pompous temple in the best 1895 beaux arts manner of Messrs. Meade, McKim, and White. It is a small oval boulder, split when it was being moved in 1774.[8] Some say it is geologically traceable to Dedham, Massachusetts, twenty miles away. It is too big to be the best way onto dry land, and too small for a jetty. Neither Bradford nor Winslow, the only two eyewitnesses who have left accounts of the various landings, mention any rock. The legend can be traced back only to the memory of a certain John Faunce, the third ruling Elder of the Plymouth congregation, who first identified the Rock in 1741 when he was in his nineties.

When the exhausted explorers arrived, *Mayflower* was still on the other side of Cape Cod Bay, and in any case had too deep a draught to get close enough to the shore to drop its passengers on to the Rock. When it did arrive, it had to be anchored more than a mile offshore.

Concerned not with history but with survival, the Pilgrims wasted no time, though they were hampered both by the weather and by the need to stop work whenever they thought there were Indians about and they had to stand to arms. On Monday, December 18, and again on Tuesday, they explored the coast. They took another look at Clark's Island, which was easy to defend, but covered with wood that would be hard to clear, and they doubted there would be fresh water in summer. So, after discussion and prayer they chose the present site of Plymouth.

It was "a high ground, where there is a great deal of land cleared and hath been planted with corn three or four years ago, and there is a very sweet brook runs under the hill side, and many delicate springs of as good water as can be drunk, and where we may harbor our shallops and boats exceeding well, and in this brook much good fish in their seasons; on the farther side of the river also much corn-ground cleared. In one field is a great hill on which we point to make a platform and plant our ordnance."[9]

The brook is Plymouth Town Brook, a shallow, babbling stream that runs pleasingly down from a series of freshwater ponds through what is now the site of Jenney's Grist Mill (a modern replica, compete with millpond, of the mill built in 1636), to a little valley, along the north side of which the Pilgrims built two rows of simple wooden houses. John Jenney, or Jenny, who came over to Plymouth in the *Little James* in July or early August 1623, was a brewer, a useful man to have in the days before water purification plants. He was given permission to build his mill "for grinding and beating of corn upon the brook of Plymouth."[10]

In February 1622 the decision was made to fortify the village. It took just over a month to surround it with a stout paling of timber, some five feet high. Myles Standish, as the only man with military experience, made them build four bulwarks, or outworks, each to be closed with a gate, but so arranged that the defenders could shoot along the walls and take attackers in flank. He also divided the able-bodied men into four companies, one for each of the gates, and he even arranged a sort of fire brigade, to protect the village if Indian attackers tried to set it alight.

In the spring of 1622, when the settlement was just over a year old, there were disquieting rumors of Indian plots to attack Plymouth. The colonists soon learned of the horrific massacre in Virginia on Good Friday (March 22, 1622, Old Style), when the Indians led by Opechancanough killed 347 English men, women, and children, or roughly one-third of the population. Already they had received a sinister warning from their own Indian neighbors. Canonicus, as the English rendered his name, sachem of the Narragansetts, sent a messenger to Plymouth. He was reluctant to say what his message was, but he left behind a bunch of arrows, wrapped in a rattlesnake's skin. It was hardly an offer of friendship.

The wooden paling included the "great hill" behind the Pilgrim's village, which is indeed so steep that you climb up it by half a dozen flights of stone stairs, is now crowned with a church and with the Pilgrims' burial ground; it is known as Burial Hill. They decided to build a fort there that would enable a small garrison to protect the town. The fort was not finished until March 1623. It took immense labor to drag half a dozen cannons, each weighing half a ton or more, up that slope. Not until then did the settlement feel truly secure.

By then the Pilgrims had survived an even more terrible test. They passed their first Christmas in America with little cheer and no feasting. As Separatist Protestants, they did not observe the

Church's traditional feasts, which they regarded as a remnant of Catholic superstition. They went on shore, some to fell, others to split timber, and "no man rested all that day." (The following year, when Thomas Weston had lumbered the colony with fifty or sixty of his irreligious recruits, without bothering to send food with them, William Bradford pointedly remembers that "on the day called Christmas Day," he called on these new recruits to work with the rest. The work-shy new arrivals said it was against their conscience to work on the holiday. When Bradford and his fellow workers came home from their tasks at noon, they found Weston's men at play. Some of them were "pitching the bar," an early version of pitching horseshoes. Others were playing "stoolball," a precursor of cricket. Very well, said Bradford, taking away their bars and bats and balls, it was against his conscience that they should play while other people were working. From that time on, Bradford recorded with what sounds like grim amusement, no one in Plymouth tried to get out of work on Christmas day, "at least openly.")

That first Christmas, the priority was to build houses. The single men were told to attach themselves to a family, so as to limit the number of houses that needed to be built, which came out at nineteen. Each person got a plot measuring eight and a quarter by forty-nine and a half feet. (The odd values are explained because the plots were measured in traditional English "rods, poles, and perches.") The houses were not log cabins, as used to be thought, but one-room frame houses with thatched roofs. In another respect, too, the settlement was different from later pioneer villages. Usually on the frontier, all the way from the Appalachians to the Rockies, the first thing settlers did was to bring as much land as they could under the plow to feed themselves. The first houses at Plymouth had gardens to grow vegetables. But the main economic activity of the colony would not be subsistence agriculture, because the Pilgrims were obligated to pay back the loans they had been given by Weston and the Adventurers. They hoped in time to be

PLYMOUTH PLANTATION
*(Photo courtesy of Plimoth Plantation, Inc., www.plimoth.org,
reprinted with permission)*

able to do that in part with fishing and lumber. But at first their only hope of earning cash was by trading with the Native Americans, and that meant above all buying beaver skins.

One day, as they worked at the houses and a "common house," as a store and a place for prayers, young Francis Billington, the same naughty boy who had nearly touched off an explosion, climbed a tree on a hill not far from the settlement and saw a body of water, which he thought was the sea. The two big joined lakes he saw are called the Billington Sea to this day.

By January the little village was in the grip of the most dangerous threat it ever faced: epidemic disease. It is not clear what form it took. Contemporary witnesses called it "the plague," but it does not seem to have been the bubonic plague. Perhaps it was tuberculosis or smallpox, or perhaps it was simply that the voyage, the exploration, exposure, not to mention the constant backbreaking work, simply left the settlers tired to death. Six, including

Bradford's wife, had already died by the end of December. Eight died in January, seventeen in February, thirteen in March, and another six later in the year. Most died of pneumonia, weakened by poor diet, possibly by scurvy, and by chills due to exposure, wading in freezing water and the bitter cold. In mid-January, the common house, in which many of the sick people were sleeping, caught fire. The thatch burned. Providentially, the barrels of gunpowder, some open, did not. The patients got out of bed to roll the barrels outside, but that only made them sicker. William Bradford described the horrors of what came to be called "the starving time."

> In the time of most distress, there was but six or seven sound persons who to their great commendations, be it spoken, spared no pains, night nor day, but with abundance of toil and hazard of their own health, fetched them wood, made them fires, dressed them meat, made their beds, washed their loathsome clothes, clothed and unclothed them. In a word, did all the homely and necessary offices for them which dainty and queasy stomachs cannot endure to hear named, and all this willingly and cheerfully, without any grudging in the least, showing herein their true love unto their friends and brethren, a rare example, and worthy to be remembered.[11]

While some behaved with true Christian courage and charity, others did not. Bradford relates that the sailors, in particular, were ungenerous when the disease first struck. When the passengers who were still sleeping on board *Mayflower* fell sick, the sailors hurried them on shore so as to conserve their stocks of beer. One sick man was roughly told by a sailor that if it was his own father he should have no beer. But when the crew, too, began to fall ill, they began to "desert one another," saying they would not risk their lives for each other. The passengers who were still on board did set an example of Christian charity, as the sailors themselves acknowledged.

All this time the Indians were "skulking about them." So when the sick died, their friends buried them at night, in secret, and covered over the site of their graves, so that the Indians should not suspect how much the settlement was weakened.

William Bradford recorded the death toll in a register of births, deaths, and punishments, which he kept in his own hand.

And in three months past, died Half our Company. The greatest part in the depth of winter, wanting houses and other comforts; being infected with the scurvy and other diseases which their long voyage and unaccommodate condition bring upon them. So as there die sometimes two or three a day. Of one hundred persons, scarce 50 remain. The living scarce able to bury the dead; the well not sufficient to tend the sick: there being in their time of greatest distress but six or seven who spare no pains to help them. Two of the seven were Master Brewster, their reverend Elder, and Master Standish the Captain. The like disease fell also among the sailors; so as almost Half their company also die, before they sail.[12]

Only twelve out of twenty-six heads of families, only four of the unattached men, and only a handful of women survived. When they were down to no more than half a dozen healthy inhabitants, the Indians could have overrun Plymouth, not without resistance, because the Pilgrims would have fought to the last man, but without difficulty. But, as we shall see, the Indians had grave troubles of their own.

One can only wonder at the courage of a group of people who survived such an appalling catalog of mortality. Any military unit, after all, which took a 50 percent casualty rate in a campaign would be withdrawn to rebuild morale and to be strengthened with new drafts. But it was to be some time before more settlers arrived in Plymouth, and the original Pilgrims had no certainty of when those reinforcements would arrive or of how many they would be. At best, the Pilgrims were no more than a few dozen men, women, and children. At the worst of the starving time they were fewer than a dozen healthy adults, perched on the rim of a continent.

CHAPTER SIX

First Encounters

O N SATURDAY, MARCH 3, THE STARVING TIME BEGAN TO end. "The wind was south," Edward Winslow recorded, "the morning misty, but towards noon warm and fair weather; the birds sang in the woods most pleasantly."[1] Then there was thunder, and heavy rain, and the weather turned cold again. But the Pilgrims were encouraged to plant some seed, as men and women who believed they might live after all. But there were still more who would die before the sickness was over. In April, Governor John Carver, who had been planting, "came out of the field very sick, it being a hot day." He lay down, and within a few hours went into some kind of coma, from which he never emerged. He died a few days later. William Bradford, who was still very ill, was chosen as his successor, and Isaac Allerton was appointed to be Bradford's assistant. On May 12, the Pilgrims celebrated a happier event, the marriage of Edward Winslow, whose wife had died in the starving time, to Susannah, widow of William White, another victim of the first bitter winter.

In the meantime, on March 16, the vulnerable Pilgrims had experienced the biggest surprise since they first landed, an event that deserves, far more than the brief, inconsequential skirmish on the beach at Eastham, to be called the First Encounter.

The Pilgrims knew very well from the start that their settlement was fragile, and that they might have to defend it at any time. They practiced military drills when they could. There is a charming glimpse of the Pilgrims marching to prayer in a letter written by a Dutch visitor, Isaack de Rasières,[2] who visited Plymouth sometime in the late 1620s.

Their houses and courtyards are arranged in very good order [he reported to a friend], with a stockade against a sudden attack; and at the ends of the streets there are three wooden gates. In the centre, on the cross street, stands the governor's house, before which is a square stockade upon which four *patereros* [small cannons] are mounted, so as to enfilade the streets. Upon the hill they have a large square house, with a flat roof . . . upon the top of which they have six cannon, which shoot iron balls of four and five pounds, and command the surrounding country. The lower part they use for their church, where they preach on Sundays and the usual holidays. They assemble by beat of drum, each with his musket or firelock, in front of the captain's door; they have their cloaks on, and place themselves in order, three abreast, and are led by a sergeant without beat of drum. Behind comes the governor, in a long robe; beside him, on the right hand, comes the preacher with his cloak on, and on the left hand the captain with his side-arms, and cloak on, and with a small cane in his hand; and so they march in good order, and each sets his arms down near him. Thus they are constantly on their guard night and day.

During the starving time, drills had been interrupted by two Indians who addressed them in sign language, but could not speak to them. In March, as the weather and their health began to improve, the Pilgrims were drilling again when a solitary Indian appeared. With the greatest boldness, he walked into the village of Plymouth, all alone, and was apparently intending to walk into the common house when they stopped him. To their amazement, he greeted them in broken English, which he had learned from the English fishermen. "Welcome," was the first English word spoken to the Pilgrims by a Native American. He was quite chatty, and reeled off the name of the captains and masters he knew who were regular visitors for the fishing, as well as the names of the various sagamores, with the number of men each could put into the field.

He wasn't a local man, but a Pemaquid chief from Monhegan, in what was later known as southern Maine, five days by land and a day's sail away with a favorable wind. He was a "tall, straight man, the hair of his head black, long behind, only short before." He was all but naked, wearing nothing but a deerskin skirt round his waist, but utterly self-confident. When the wind rose and it became a little chilly, they gave him a red horseman's coat to wear. He asked for beer. Instead they gave him strong liquor, with ship's biscuit, butter, cheese, and pudding, and a piece of mallard duck, all of which he liked.

The Pilgrims talked to this surprise visitor all afternoon. They wanted to get rid of him before night, but he did not want to go. So then they thought of taking him out to *Mayflower*, which was standing offshore, and he was happy to go along with that. They got him into the shallop, but the wind was too high and the tide was out, so they had to give up that idea, and lodged him in Stephen Hopkins' house instead.

He told them a good deal about the local Indians. There were only about sixty warriors of Massasoit, he said, that is of the Wampanoags of Massasoit's village, and no more than a hundred of the Nausets on Cape Cod, with whom the Pilgrims had already had their skirmish. The Nausets and the Wampanoags were both angry with the English, the Indian visitor said, because of Captain Hunt. He had pretended to want to trade with them. Instead, he took twenty of the Wampanoags and seven of the Nausets prisoner by trickery and sold them as slaves in Spain for twenty pounds a man.

The visitor—he said his name was Samoset—turned out to know a good deal about the Pilgrims. He knew about the fight at First Encounter Beach. And he knew about some tools the Wampanoags had stolen, which the Pilgrims angrily asked him to return.

The next morning, a Saturday, they sent Samoset away with some presents: a knife, a bracelet, and a ring. He promised to come back with some of Massasoit's men, and some beaver skins to trade. On Sunday, Samoset came back with five other Indians, "tall, proper men." They wore long leather hose, almost to the groin, and the same little skirt Samoset had worn, and they all wore deerskins except for the leader, who wore the skin of a wildcat. They ate English food, but they had also brought some food of their own, corn flour in a receptacle like a bow case. And their leader had some tobacco, which the others smoked only when he gave them the sign. Their faces were smeared with black paint. It was clear that they wanted to be friendly. They put on a show of singing and dancing, which reminded Winslow of clowns—"antics," he called them—he had seen in Europe. And they returned the stolen tools. They wanted to barter a few beaver skins. But it was Sunday, and the Pilgrims would not do business on the Sabbath, and got rid of the Indians as soon as they could.

They went, but Samoset stayed behind, until the following Wednesday, when they sent him away, so that they could get on with discussing some important questions: There were laws and regulations to be framed, and some military orders to be given. But once again, while they were debating these matters on the top of the hill where they kept the cannon, two Indians showed up and made aggressive gestures with their bows and arrows. So Captain Standish took two of the Pilgrims and two of the sailors from *Mayflower*, with muskets, and the Indians ran away.

The following day, once more warm and fair, the Pilgrims had only been discussing their affairs for an hour when Samoset turned up again, and this time he brought with him the only surviving native of Patuxet, as the Indians called Plymouth. His name was Tisquantum, or Squanto. He was one of the twenty Wampanoags who had been kidnapped by Captain Hunt and taken to Spain, and somehow he had managed to find his way to London, where he lodged in Cornhill with a merchant called Master John Slanie. As a result he spoke English, not perfectly, but better than Samoset. Samoset and Squanto brought some goodwill offerings, a few skins and some fresh red herring. It took them some time to explain their message, which was that the great king of the Wampanoags, Massasoit, and his brother Quadrequina, were near at hand with all their men.

After a while it became clear enough what was happening, because Massasoit and his sixty warriors appeared on the top of a nearby hill. The Pilgrims were not prepared to risk sending their governor to talk to the king, and the king was not prepared to come to them. So Edward Winslow was chosen as a sort of ambassador. He took with him a pair of knives, a copper chain with a jewel fastened to it, and a pot of hard liquor.

It was an edgy, suspicious occasion. Winslow made a speech, translated by Squanto, to the effect that King James saluted Massasoit with words of love and peace, and that the governor of Plymouth wanted to see Massasoit, and trade with him, and agree to a treaty. Massasoit was pleased with the speech, and offered to buy Winslow's sword and armor, but Winslow was not ready to go that far. So he was consigned to Quadrequina, the king's brother, while Massasoit descended from his hill, and crossed the shallow Town Brook with twenty braves, where Standish met him with half a dozen musketeers. The Pilgrims kept half a dozen of the Indians as hostages for Winslow, and escorted Massasoit to an empty house that was still being built, where they ensconced him on a green rug. He was a vigorous man, in the prime of life, with a bag of white bones as his regalia, a little bag of tobacco hanging down his back, and a long knife hanging by a thong round his neck. He was nervous: He shook with something like fear all the time the parley continued.

The governor, John Carver, arrived with ceremony and an escort of musketeers. A drummer and a trumpet announced his presence and his importance. The Indians were fascinated by the trumpet, and some of them tried, without much success, to get a sound out of it. The high contracting parties kissed hands, for all the world as if they were two brother sovereigns of Europe greeting one another with diplomatic protocol before sitting down to swap half a dozen provinces. Then Carver called for strong liquor, French brandy perhaps or Dutch Geneva, and drank to the Indian's health, and Massasoit returned the compliment by drinking so much of the raw spirit that it made him sweat visibly for a long while.

After which solemn preliminaries, they duly agreed on a pact of peace and nonaggression. Massasoit agreed not to injure the English, and if any of his men disobeyed that agreement, he would send them to the English to be punished, and he would return any tools that might be stolen. The English, for their part, agreed to help the Indian if anyone made war on him, and he agreed to help them if any other Indians attacked them. On that basis, said Carver, King James, by the grace of God, Lord of England, Scotland, and Ireland (not to mention France, to which English kings had laid claim since the fourteenth century!) would count Massasoit of the Wampanoags as his right trusty friend and ally.

IT WAS ON THE WHOLE A TREATY FAVORABLE TO THE ENGLISH. Even at the time, Winslow understood that the reason why the chief of the Wampanoags was willing to seek the friendship of the Plymouth colonists was because he thought he might need their support against his Native American rivals, and especially against his archenemy, Corbitant, the sachem of the powerful Narragansetts. Their territory was in what was to become Rhode Island, to the west of the Wampanoag territory. But the Pilgrims could hardly have been expected to understand the broader strategic facts of their situation, and of their Indian neighbors.

It is natural for us, almost four centuries later, to fit the relationship between English settlers and Native Americans into one or the other of two narratives, both wrong or at least oversimple. Either we see the Indians as poor, naked "savages," doomed to be all but exterminated by the superior technology, morale, and numbers of the European settlers. Or, alternatively, one can empathize with a tiny band of English men, women, and children, all but exterminated by disease themselves and pathetically vulnerable to fierce Indian warriors, clinging by their fingernails to the rim of the continent. After all, half the 102 members of the Pilgrim party who had crossed the ocean were dead by the time Samoset appeared: At Jamestown, only thirty-eight out of the first 108 colonists survived the first winter,[3] and in March of 1622 a series of Indian attacks, carefully coordinated by the Pamunkey Chief Opechancanough, killed at least 330 English people, perhaps one-quarter to one-third of the colony's population.[4]

Neither of those two schemes accurately represents the situation of the first years after the Plymouth settlement. The fact is that both the English and Indians were desperately weak and vulnerable. Like two battered, old pro fighters, in the intervals of combat they propped one another up. Later, things changed. With the immigration to Massachusetts Bay after 1629, massive by comparison, the balance of power shifted decisively in favor of the

English. But at first they both needed each other, and they were aware that they needed each other.

There were survival skills that the Indians could teach the English. Very early on, to take one example, the Indians taught the English to plant a dead fish at the root of each corn plant, to supply calcium and other nutrients; after all, the English were completely unfamiliar with what they called "Indian corn." The Indians, too, had much to teach about how to find the seafood that added so much to the quality of their own diet, especially clams and eels. They were expert trackers and woodsmen, leatherworkers, and potters. The English, too, of course, brought technology with them, including some very simple technology that had been known in Europe for centuries, as well as the more spectacular technology of sailing ships, which the Indians called "floating islands," and their superior, if cumbersome, musketry and cannon. (The Indians were of course very skillful with their bows, which could shoot off many arrows in the time it took a seventeenth-century European to load and fire a musket.) The Indians especially valued European knives, axes, fishhooks, and other tools, as well they might after centuries of trying to tame the wilderness with blades made from copper or from seashells.

It is striking that some aspects of Indian culture that came to be thought of as typical, had in fact been introduced, or at least substantially changed, by Europeans. The classic example of this is wampum. For many centuries, perhaps millennia, the Algonquian-speaking peoples of Quebec, Maine, and southern New England had valued beads made from the shells of clams, whelks, and other mollusks. By the early seventeenth century, these beads could be strung together in elaborate and beautiful belts, which meant far more than the "Indian money" they were sometimes called by Europeans. Wampum was "a means of exchange and a store of value." But it also had cultural value of many other kinds: as decoration, as art, as a symbol in diplomatic and even religious contexts. Yet wampum beads, in what became their classic form, were impossible until the Native Americans could use European steel awls to bore holes in the material. Only then could they be strung together in long sequences or belts.

Native American people quickly adapted and used European sailing techniques. Early settlers soon saw them using European-style shirts as sails for their canoes, and one of the very earliest European explorers of the Maine coast was startled to find Indians skillfully sailing a "Baskeshallop," that is, a Basque sailing boat they had obtained from Basque fishermen in Newfoundland or Cape Breton.[5]

The underlying reason for Native American vulnerability was epidemic disease. Everywhere in the Americas, European settlers brought with them diseases to which they had acquired immunity by being exposed since childhood, but which were devastatingly lethal in populations without that immunity. That was true in the Caribbean in the early 1500s, in Quebec and New England in the early 1600s, and in the Missouri valley and the Great Plains in the 1800s. It remained true when the native peoples of the remotest corners of the Amazon basin and Alaska were exposed to contact with Europeans as late as the twentieth century.

Historians and epidemiologists argue over the scale of the depopulation brought by syphilis, influenza, measles, chickenpox, smallpox, and the plague in different parts of the Americas at different times. It has been estimated that there may have been twenty-five million Native Americans in the territories of New Spain when Columbus landed, and that by the end of the sixteenth century they had dwindled to fewer than two million. It is clear that the devastation, especially as a result of smallpox, was particularly appalling among the New England Indians, where it was very recent when the Pilgrims staggered ashore on Clark's island in Plymouth Bay.

SAMOSET AND SQUANTO—LIKE MOST NATIVE AMERICAN peoples—were people not without history, but without written history. To reconstruct their experience before their disastrous contact with the Europeans is therefore hard. It has to be pieced together from those sources that are available, and—even more than is usually the case—these are both scarce and unreliable.

Existing archeological evidence includes settlement sites, burial finds and physical relics such as weapons, jewels, and ceramics. Native Americans have left behind rich, if from a historian's point of view somewhat puzzling, oral traditions. Sometimes, for example, a tribe has preserved a strong tradition that it had migrated from elsewhere at some point in historic time, but without any precision about when, let alone why, these movements took place. Most dangerous of all for modern historians are the accounts of Europeans who met Native Americans in one way or another before European dominance had been established. Sometimes this happened through capture. European capture of Indians, some of whom were taken to Europe to be exhibited as exotic prizes or as evidence of voyages or conquests made, was more common than Indian capture of Europeans. Many of these European captives were killed, often after horrible torture. But others were well treated and returned through some accident or another to European society. Sometimes they seem to have given up their Indian life reluctantly. But in all these cases, European narratives of Indian life have to be taken with a pinch of salt, if only because captives rarely saw more than a tiny segment of Indian life. "I have observed," wrote a shrewd French Jesuit as early as 1633, "that after seeing two or three Savages do the same thing, it is at once reported to be a custom of the whole Tribe."[6] All these kinds of evidence about the native societies into which Europeans stumbled in the sixteenth and early seventeenth centuries are vague and more or less unreliable. All, until relatively recently, have been colored by European, and later white American, prejudices and fears.

Even so, especially in recent decades, scholars have established enough for us to be able to know quite a lot about the native peoples of North America. Some of the most important facts of which we can be fairly sure are negative facts. The Native Americans, for one thing, were not newcomers. They had, most scholars agree, originally traveled from East Asia by way of the Bering land bridge. (Many Native Americans dispute this, mainly on the grounds that their religious traditions teach that they were always present in North America.) They had in any case been living in coastal northeastern North America for between ten thousand and forty thousand years.[7] They were far from being all the same: they had different customs, different beliefs, different identities. They spoke many languages, of several language groups. Some were hunters, other agriculturalists, many were both. A few, at various times in the past, lived in quite large cities. Others lived in small villages.

They were, until the arrival of the European diseases against which they had no immunity, remarkably healthy. "Take them when the blood is briske in their veines, said one seventeenth-century observer,[8] "when the flesh is on their backs, and marrow in their bones, when they frolick in their antique deportments and Indian postures . . . they are more amiable to behold (though only in Adam's livery)" than Europeans in the latest fashions. Their diet was excellent, and their health seems to have been good. They wore a minimum of clothes, but protected themselves from cold, insect bites, and so on with a thick layer of fat or grease. This may have made them smelly at close quarters, though hardly smellier than the Europeans, who changed their clothes rarely.

Although it is impossible to be sure how many Native American people there were in North America when the Europeans arrived, it is certain that the land the Pilgrims entered was not teeming with people. One estimate is that there have been about two Indians to every ten square miles. That was a far cry from Elizabethan England, where over four million people were already crowded into ninety thousand square miles. Other parts of Europe, notably Holland, the Spanish Netherlands (modern Belgium), and northern Italy were more or less equally populous.

Understandably, in the case of people who depended even more than their European contemporaries on nature, the Native American way of life was dramatically affected by climate change. And there was a substantial change in the North American climate in historic time. Between about the middle of the tenth century and the middle of the fourteenth there was a relatively warm period. Climatologists call it "the medieval optimum." It was this warmer weather that allowed Norse adventurers to colonize Greenland and visit Newfoundland and the St. Lawrence region. In the North American southeast and the Mississippi valley, it made possible a wealthy and sophisticated society reminiscent in some ways of the river cultures of the Indus valley, Mesopotamia, and Egypt with their rigidly subordinated societies.

In the Archaic and Woodland periods, Native American communities constructed mounds, used mainly to bury the dead, as early as 8000 or even 9000 BC. By about AD 800 , these mounds, in river valleys including those of the Ohio, the Black Warrior, the Arkansas, and especially the Mississippi, developed into towns that traded with one another over a wide area. The mound sites changed. Round burial mounds were replaced by flat-topped platforms. An elite buried their dead but also built homes on the top of these large mounds. In front of, or between, these mounds there were open parade grounds or plazas where religious events were staged.

The growth of towns was made possible by collecting food from the surrounding countryside, presumably by force, and by an agricultural revolution that improved the diet. This took the form of improved culture of two crops, corn and squash, and the arrival of a new crop, beans. New strains of corn with a short growing cycle made two harvests a season possible, and also made it possible to farm higher up river valleys. The "three sisters" of Indian diet—corn, squash, and beans—reinforced one another in ways modern biologists have been able to explain. Beans are a source of the amino acids lysine and tryptophan. Combined with the chief amino acid in corn, zein, they produce a nutritious protein. Squash is an excellent source of vitamins. Taken together, the three crops have a nutritional value greater than the sum of their parts.

Roughly between AD 1200 and AD 1400 was the heyday of the Mississippian culture. During this relatively warm age, the Native Americans of North America, from Wisconsin to the mouth of the Mississippi, and from eastern Texas to north Georgia and west Florida, developed in the great river valleys an urban culture with some resemblances to the civilization of Aztec Mexico, though most scholars believe it developed independently. The Mississippian culture built large cities like Cahokia—near the present East St. Louis, and estimated to have had a population of more than twenty thousand—and the other "mound" cities of Mississippi, Alabama, and Georgia. The largest of more than one hundred mounds in Cahokia, Monk's Mound, covers an area of some fifteen acres. It rises in four terraces to a height of one hundred feet, on top of which the palace of the ruler would have risen another fifty feet. The "city" had an area of about five square miles, and the central district, including public markets, specialized buildings including granaries, saunas, and lodges for menstruating women, was defended by a massive stockade of oak and hickory logs. At the center of Cahokia, there were several circles of pits that contained huge red cedar posts. Scholars believe these constituted a form of solar calendar used for astronomical and religious purposes.

Smaller but still imposing mound settlements were built in many other places in the Mississippi valley and the southeast. Among them were Moundville, on the Black Warrior River about fifteen miles south of Tuscaloosa, Alabama, and Etowah, in Georgia, some thirty miles northwest of Atlanta.

These were highly sophisticated but also sharply stratified societies. A priestly elite ruled over an elite of commoners who included traders, warriors, and craftsmen, and the urban populations were fed by agricultural villages. (This resembles the fourfold division that is at the basis of the Indian caste system, between *brahmins* (priests); *kshatriya* (warriors); *vaishya* (traders and cultivators); and *shudra* (workers).) At the apex, rulers, who were also priests of a religion of sun worship, performed ceremonies celebrating the power and beneficence of the sun and tracing the movements of the solar system. These priest-kings cemented their own power by leading elaborate rituals and by distributing to the populace ritual objects that symbolized the sun and the harvest cycle.

Some time before Columbus reached the West Indies in 1492 the climate got colder. A "Little Ice Age" took the place of the climatic optimum. The great mound cities collapsed, and their populations were dispersed. By 1600, the Mississippian civilization no longer existed. We don't know exactly how that happened. Climate change is accepted as the fundamental cause of its disappearance, but climate change is gradual. Probably changes in the weather caused food shortages, which in turn caused social unrest, leading to uprisings, rebellions, and flight from the mound cities and towns. Quite possibly the subject people, not to mention the slaves, had little to lose by overthrowing the priest-rulers.

Little is known about the detail of the resulting population movements. It is thought that the people who spoke the Muskogean group of languages, which includes the Choctaw, Chickasaw, Creek, and Seminole languages, are the descendants of the Mississippian mound builders. In any case, Algonquian-speaking peoples spread south from their original home in eastern Canada out west to the Plains (Arapaho) and down the coast of New England. They were split, however, by the thrust of the Iroquois-speaking peoples, who included the Seneca, Huron, and Mohawk in the north and the Cherokee in the south.

The Iroquois confederacy was founded in the fourteenth or fifteenth century, or perhaps as early as the twelfth, by the personage who was the historical model for Henry Wadsworth Longfellow's Hiawatha. It consisted of the five nations (Mohawks, Oneida, Onondaga, Cayuga, and Seneca from east to west) living in western New York state, roughly from Albany to Buffalo by way of the Finger Lakes. (In the eighteenth century they accepted the Tuscarora from western North Carolina as the sixth nation in their confederacy.) They were proud of the unwritten constitution of the confederacy. Altogether in the seventeenth century the Iroquois totaled some twelve thousand people, which would have made them one of the strongest groupings, as they were certainly among the fiercest warriors, at the time. They later exterminated their enemies the Huron.

The Native American people throughout the United States were divided into tribes, few them counting more than a few thousand members. Each tribe was ruled by a sachem, or sagamore, supported by powwows (shamans or medicine men in this sense, although also meaning "a gathering"). The chiefdoms were hereditary, but in most, not all, cases they descended through the female line. The sachems had a general authority over the tribal lands, analogous to the feudal overlordship of a medieval European king. Under this, subtribes and families owned land in full possession, and were well aware of the boundaries of their land, whether it was used for agriculture or hunting, though sachems frequently tried to help themselves to tribal and family land. These tribes were typically divided into subtribes of related families. Every tribe, and in fact every subtribe also, owned tribal lands. These were theoretically permanent homes, although there was a good deal of raiding and border fighting.

The Algonquian-speaking inhabitants of what was to become New England called themselves the Ninnimissinuok. The northernmost were the Abnaki, sometimes called by the English and other Indians the "Tarrantines." They were a warlike tribe, some three thousand strong, constrained by the hardness of the winter to live more by hunting than agriculture to a greater degree than tribes further south. They lived in the present Maine, between the Piscataqua river on the New Hampshire line north and east to Penobscot. Then, moving south and west, came the Pennacooks. Further inland, in western Massachusetts, were the Nipmucks, a weak tribe often obliged to pay tribute or hand over territory to other Indians. West of them were the Pocumtucks, a loose association of bands centered on Deerfield, in western Massachusetts. Further west again, in southern Vermont and on the upper Hudson, lived the Mahicans, menaced from the west by the fierce Mohawks.

Returning to the coast, the Massachusetts tribe lived around the bay of that name. By 1630 they numbered no more than five hundred, which may explain their relatively welcoming attitude to the English settlers. South of them were the Pilgrims' neighbors the Wampanoags, and on Cape Cod the Nausets, some twelve hundred of them. The Wampanoags, as we have seen, were so badly hit by the epidemic of 1616–18 that part of their territory was abandoned. Some of their dozen or more subtribes inhabited Martha's Vineyard and the other islands, but their sachem's capital was at Pokanoket, on the present site of Bristol, Rhode Island. There is a theory that the Wampanoags had been so badly hit by disease that Massasoit, or Osamequin, the sachem with whom the Pilgrims concluded their treaty of peace, actually created what amounted to a new tribe out of scattered survivors of the epidemic.

To the west of Narragansett Bay, in modern Rhode Island, were the Narragansetts, the bitter enemies of the Wampanoag, led by their chiefs Canonicus and Miantonomo. Although the English settlers described them as the least warlike of the New England tribes, modern historians think otherwise. There were about four thousand of them, and they were left relatively unharmed by the 1616 epidemic. Beyond them in eastern Connecticut lived the Pequots, which means the "destroyers," a branch of the Mahicans of the upper Hudson River valley. For some reason, perhaps as a result of the rise of the Iroquois confederacy, they pushed southward with brutality. The Mohawks were even more dangerous. "Their ferocity in war, their early acquisition of firearms, and their frequent raids to the east," writes the historian of the New England frontier,[9] "had given the Mohawks an unsavory reputation even before the Puritans came." Both other Indians and Europeans were shocked by their reputation for cannibalism.

The eastern half of Long Island, the land of the Montauk tribe, was considered in the seventeenth century to be part of Connecticut, and therefore of New England. Power over the Montauks was disputed by the Narragansetts and the Pequots, among others.

The New England Indians were not nomads. While older historians portray them as essentially hunters, contemporary European accounts clearly support the judgment of Francis Jennings that, "among the east coast tribes south of Maine hunting was a supplementary activity in a predominately agricultural or, to be precise, horticultural economy." Typically the Indians of New England had not one but at least three more or less settled homes. They would have a winter home, often in an upper valley, where they would build solid longhouses forty, fifty, or even a hundred feet long. A summer home by the sea allowed them to supplement their diet by fishing, and took the form of movable round or oval wigwams. (They built their houses by bending branches to form a dome, then covering the frame with mats, bark, or skins.) The inside of a wigwam was lined with woven mats, and a low platform, twelve- to eighteen-inches high, ran round the interior for sleeping or sitting. Wigwams were often both smoky and infested with vermin.[10]

In spring, the Indians often moved to the fall line of the rivers, so as to take advantage of the run of fish swimming upriver to breed.[11] And in late autumn they might move to a hunting camp to accumulate meat for the winter. Being without salt or vinegar, it was hard for them to preserve the deer, moose, and beaver meat they killed except by drying it. Indians, and especially Indian women, were skillful gardeners. They planted corn, beans, and squash in the same hills. Bean vines climbed the corn stalks, and their nodules fertilized the soil with nitrates, while squash plants kept away weeds. This culture produced high yields for relatively little work. Women also picked fruit, wild berries, and herbs for cooking and medicinal use. The men hunted, not only with bow and arrow but also with snares, like the one that tripped up William Bradford on Cape Cod and elaborate tunnel traps into which they could drive big game such as deer and moose—the Pilgrims stumbled across one of those on Cape Cod too.

No one knows exactly how many Native Americans inhabited New England in the sixteenth century. One expert estimate is that there were between 70,000 and 144,000 native people in southern New England in 1600, of whom between 17,600 and 37,600 were to be found in what is now eastern Massachusetts.[12] All the tribes from Newfoundland down to Connecticut had been living there for at least ten thousand years, and, according to some recent scholarship, much longer than that. They all spoke different dialects of the Algonquian language.

Although we think of European settlement as beginning with the unsuccessful colony at Roanoke in the North Carolina outer banks in the 1580s, with Jamestown after 1607 and Plymouth in 1620, by then Europeans were no new sight on the North Atlantic coast. The first fishermen from Bristol may have appeared in Newfoundland and discovered the wealth of the Grand Banks fisheries as early as the 1480s, when they took several dozen Micmac Indians prisoner and carried them back to England. John Cabot took possession of Newfoundland in the name of King Henry VII of England after landing there in 1497.

Throughout the sixteenth century, English, Breton, Basque, Portuguese, Norman, and Dutch boats fished the Grand Banks and established drying stations where they salted the cod and other species in Labrador and Newfoundland. They also caught whales. When *Mayflower* anchored in Provincetown Bay, the sight of whales playing in the shallow waters of the Stellwagen shelf immediately suggested a profitable enterprise to Edward Winslow. "Every day we saw whales playing hard by us, of which in that place, if we had instruments and means to take them, we might have made a very rich return, which to our great grief we wanted. Our master and his mate, and others experienced in fishing, professed we might have made three or four thousand pounds' worth of oil." They said it looked more profitable than whaling in Greenland.

By 1580 it is estimated that anything from three hundred fifty to seven hundred boats, manned by eight thousand to ten thousand Europeans, spent every summer fishing on the American side of the North Atlantic. As the century ended, they were beginning to work their way further south, through Maine to Cape Cod. That was how it came about that the Pilgrims met English-speaking Indians like Samoset and Squanto. Contact, including sexual contact, between Europeans and Native Americans, had been going on for decades, indeed generations, when the first colonists arrived. But by a painful irony it was the innocent children who came with settlers, but were rarely found on fishing boats, who were most likely to bring the viral diseases of childhood, so that epidemic disease accelerated after settlement had begun.

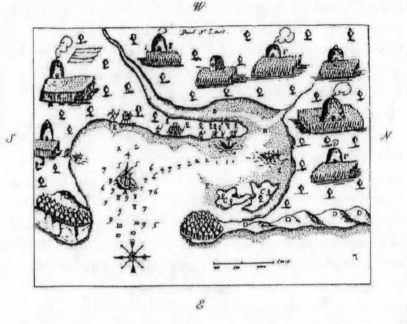

CHAMPLAIN'S MAP
*(Illustration courtesy of the John Carter Brown Library at Brown University,
reprinted with permission)*

In 1604 the French explorer Samuel de Champlain not only visited the site, which he called Port St. Louis, where the Pilgrims were to found Plymouth sixteen years later,[13] but drew a remarkably accurate map, showing the Town Brook running down behind the long bar of Plymouth Beach and the shape of Clark's Island and Saquish Head. There is something even more remarkable about Champlain's map, however. It clearly shows Indian huts with fires smoking, surrounded by gardens, fields of corn, and cleared forest—and Indians, plenty of them.

In 1616 this thriving community was literally wiped off Champlain's map by an epidemic. Probably for the reason given above—the greater number of European children arriving—the evidence suggests that these diseases did not have much impact in the North Atlantic region until after 1600. That changed swiftly as fishermen and explorers gave way to settlers with families. Within a year of the French settling at Port Royal in 1610, for example, three-quarters of the local tribe, the Micmacs, were dead, killed by epidemics.[14]

A major epidemic broke out in 1616 and lasted until 1619. It is not clear whether it was smallpox or some other disease, such as chicken pox or hepatitis. The results were devastating. It spread from the Penobscot River in Maine all the way down the present coasts of Maine, New Hampshire, Massachusetts, and Rhode Island to the eastern shore of Narragansett Bay. The Abnaki, Massachusetts, Wampanoags, and Narragansetts were all affected. "I passed along the Coast," wrote Dermer, "where I found some antient Plantations [i.e. settlements], not long since populous, now utterly void; in other places a remnant remains, but not free of sickness." Dermer's sponsor, Sir Ferdinando Gorges, reported that the native Americans were "Sore afflicted with the Plague, for that country was in a manner left void of inhabitants."[15] The Pilgrim Robert Cushman, who visited Plymouth in 1621, calculated that "the twentieth person is scarce left alive." When the Pilgrims arrived in 1620, the Wampanoags had been almost unimaginably devastated by an epidemic that struck the New England coast from 1616 to 1618. Before the epidemic, the population of the area around Cape Cod, Martha's Vineyard, and Nantucket may have had fifteen thousand people; by 1619 it had one thousand. The Massachusetts were even worse struck than the Wampanoags, but the Narragansetts escaped almost unscathed and were able to force the Wampanoags to cede them territory, which in itself explains the eagerness of the Wampanoag chief to get the Pilgrims on his side.[16]

Epidemics were not the only cause of pressure on the Indian way of life or of depopulation. For one thing, some Indian tribes, such as the Mohawks, deliberately set out to replenish military strength lost to epidemics by raiding to seize captives from neighboring tribes and recruit them forcibly to their ranks. For another,

European agriculture, both arable and pastoral, demanded land. In the early years of settlement, the Pilgrims, like other European settlers, allowed pigs in particular to roam far and wide in the woods, where they ate much of the food that used to sustain bears, deer, and the other game the Indians hunted. Pigs and cattle also fed on the unfenced fields where the Indians raised corn, squash, and beans, the staples of their diet. The fur trade, too, destroyed Indian game. Beavers had played an important part in Indian agriculture because their dams and ponds helped to create cultivable land and created pockets of fertility where the Indians could grow crops. Beaver dams trapped soil runoff. They slowed river flow, with a resulting increase in water temperature, which increased insect and plankton life and encouraged fish and water birds. Disused beaver dams created rich alluvial soils. After about 1640 the fur trade in New England died away. Trappers had to travel further west to find furs as beaver became scarce in the northeast.

Now it was beavers the English and, farther north, the French coveted above everything, and needed to send home to pay off their debts. Miantonomo, a Narragansett chief, summed up the whole disastrous process in 1642:

> Our fathers had plenty of deer and skins, our plains were full of deer, as also our woods, and of turkeys, and our coves full of fish and fowl. But these English having gotten our land, they with scythes cut down the grass, and with axes fell the trees; their cows and horses eat the grass, and their hogs spoil our clam banks, and we shall all be starved.[17]

Enthusiasts for colonization took the apparently miraculous wave of Indian mortality as clear evidence that God approved of their designs for settlement. Thomas Hariot believed it was "the speciall worke of God for our sakes." Gorges wrote that "there hath by God's Visitation, raigned a wonderfull Plague." John

Winthrop, the patron saint of American exceptionalism, was asked "what warrant have we to take that lande which is and hathe been of long tyme possessed by other sonnes of Adam." He replied "God hath consumed the natives with a miraculous plague, where by a great parte of the Country is left voyde of Inhabitantes." And this view had the official imprimatur of no less a personage than King James. The patent the king granted to Gorges for the Virginia Company in November 1620 (while the Pilgrims were actually nearing Cape Cod) stated that

> We in our judgment are persuaded and satisfied that the appointed Time is come in which Almighty God in his great Goodness and Bountie toward Us and our People hath thought fit and determined, that those large and goodly Territoryes, deserted as it were by their naturall Inhabitants, should be possessed and enjoyed by such of our Subject and People.[18]

It is good to be able to report that it was one thing for courtiers and promoters in London to see the horrible sufferings of the Indians as evidence of the hand of God and as a bull point for investment, quite another for men and women on the spot to be indifferent to those sufferings which Thomas Hariot later compared to a "Golgotha."

For one thing, the first English settlers in North America were not racist, at least in the minimum sense that they never had any doubt that Native Americans were humans like themselves. True, they frequently described them by abusive terms, such as "savages" or "barbarians." They often told stories about the Indians' supposed cruelty, though contemporary European executions and the way victorious armies behaved in, for example, Germany, the Balkans, or Ireland in the seventeenth century show that sadism was scarcely an Indian monopoly. But they did not think the Indians were subhuman. "No one who had actually been to America ever believed anything of the kind. All agreed that Indians met the test; they lived in civil society. That implied a complex language, hereditary government, organization of society in towns and agriculture that implied care to provide for the morrow."[19] On the contrary, travelers' accounts, and not only those of the godly Pilgrims, often pointed out how physically strong, healthy, and beautiful Indians were—before, that is, they were infected with disease. John Brereton, one of the earliest explorers, thought that the Indians' "perfect constitution" was shown in their strength, agility, and straight posture. Thomas Morton, who explored southern New England, said of them that "they are as proper men and women for features and limbes as can be found, for flesh and bloud as active."

On the whole the early English explorers did not see the Indians as born with naturally different colored skin. Indians were never said to be red in this early period; they were almost always described as tanned or tawny. Some English observers, like Captain John Smith, believed that Indians "are borne white." "Their swarthiness," wrote another, William Wood, of native New England tribes, "is the Sun's livery, for they are borne faire." Others wrote that the natives were tawny "not by nature but accidentally," because they learned that the Indians stained their skin with walnut juice and other vegetable dyes because it protected them from mosquitoes and other biting insects. Early European travelers also admired the way Indians, especially of "the better sort," decorated their bodies. George Percy, younger brother of the earl of Northumberland, which made him undeniably one of the "better sort" by contemporary standards among the English in Virginia, liked the way some Indians "paint their bodies blacke, some red, with artificial knots of sundry lively colours, very beautiful and pleasing to the eye." Percy thought the followers of the chief of the Rappahannock were "as goodly men as any I have seen, of Savages or Christians."[20]

The English assumed that the Native Americans came from a common stock of humans. In the early years, Roger Williams was not alone in his opinion that, "Nature knowes no difference between Europe and Americans in blood, birth, bodies and &c God having of one blood made all mankind, Acts 17 and all by nature being children of wrath, Ephesians 12. . . . Boast not proud English. . . . Thy brother Indian is by birth as Good."[21]

The English did not encounter the Native Americans with a generalized racial contempt. But as the Europeans grew in number and pressed harder and harder on the Indians' lands and their way of life, relations deteriorated. Whether or not tragedy was inevitable, it was not long in coming.

Before that happened, however, sometime in the fall of 1621 there took place that curious encounter that came erroneously to be known as the First Thanksgiving.

CHAPTER SEVEN

The Loss of Trust

THE IDEA OF A FIRST THANKSGIVING SHARED EQUALLY between native Indians and newly arrived settlers benignly exaggerated a relatively insignificant encounter—the improvised backwoods diplomacy—so that it became a dominant event in the national narrative. This image of the First Thanksgiving seems to legitimize the arrival of the settlers because of the cooperative and nurturing quality of the event. It is almost something out of Eden: At inception, the venture finds bounty in a shared feast with the natives. You could hardly ask for a more promising image with which to begin the great adventure of spreading your faith into a new and vast continent. But in truth, this idea of the First Thanksgiving is camouflage for the reality of the Pilgrims' first years. They were hard times, for Pilgrims and Indians alike.

The circumstances, especially the immediate past that had assailed the Wampanoag—so recently shattered by the impact of epidemics brought by the arriving Europeans—helps to explain why the Indian tribes saw the Europeans not as enemies of the entire Native American population but as potential allies. Native American society was riven with conflicts, some bitter and bloody, over land, security, and supremacy, the eternal sources of war in all human societies. Every tribe had at least one hereditary enemy. The Wampanoags wanted to make peace with the Pilgrims in part because they hoped to use them and their guns against the Narragansetts and the Massachusetts. In the beginning, the English were just another tribe. In numbers, at first, they were neither more nor less threatening than any other Indian tribe.

In the early years, therefore, there was no automatic enmity between Englishmen and Indians as such, though there was certainly mutual suspicion. The Indians did not start out by hating the English, though they resented their hunger for land and the way they and their animals behaved on the lands they occupied. The English saw the Indians as human, not subhuman, and they made an effort to deal with them fairly and to convert them to their God; but that did not stop them calling them "savages" or taking it for granted that they were inferiors. Even those of the English most friendly towards the Indians spoke of them contemptuously. Daniel Gookin, who worked with them, believed they were "not many degrees above beasts in matters of fact."[1] John Eliot, who devoted his life to converting them, called them "the dregs and ruins of mankind," and even Roger Williams, their greatest champion, called them "barbarous scum and offscourings of mankinde."[2]

However, in general, the English settlers, in the early years, were careful to treat the Native Americans with fairness. They punished Englishmen for common-law crimes against Indians as if they had been committed against other Englishmen. One John Dawe was whipped for "enticing an Indian woman to lie with him," and Nicholas Frost was fined, whipped, branded on the hand, and banished for stealing from the Indians. Even Sir Richard Saltonstall, one of the grandees of the Massachusetts Bay colony, was twice punished for allowing his servants to damage Indian property. It did not occur to the English to think this was arrogant on their part. They took it for granted that their charters gave them authority over the "savages." But they also thought their laws should protect them equally. And this was only enlightened self-interest in the first period of settlement, when the colonies were plainly vulnerable to Indian attack. The result was that Indians were quite willing to offer land for sale to the Europeans to buy their tempting and useful goods. The Europeans were in general rather scrupulous in buying, rather than simply appropriating, land. They recognized three titles to land: patent, possession, and purchase.

The English, though, were not willing to share everything. They realized how important their monopoly of firearms was to their safety. They therefore tried to forbid selling guns to the Indians, but with only partial success. When Thomas Morton, a very un-Puritan lawyer who set up the maypole at his riotous colony of "Merrymount," at Mount Wollaston, Massachusetts, which upset Governor Bradford by encouraging "dancing and frisking together (like so many fairies or furies rather) and worse practises"[3] was found to be selling firearms to the Indians—the Pilgrims intervened at once. They sent in Miles Standish, who found the merry colonists drunk, arrested them, brought them back to Plymouth under armed guard, and shipped them back to England. Bradford wrote to the Council for New England asking them to help control the arms trade, "otherwise we shall be forced to quit the country to our great grief and dishonor to our nation; for we shall be beaten with our own arms if we abide."

The Massachusetts Bay Company, from its arrival, was very strict in this respect. In September 1630, the Court passed a law forbidding the use of guns by Indians even if they were hunting as servants of Englishmen. Although this prohibition was relaxed for the governor and one or two other high officials, the penalties imposed for selling firearms to Indians were severe. In 1632 a certain Richard Hopkins was whipped and branded on the cheek for selling guns, powder, and shot to an Indian chief, and there was serious discussion of the death penalty. Yet these attempts were in vain.

Before long firearms were common enough in the Indian villages, and when open war came between Indians and Englishmen in the 1670s, the Indians were as well accustomed to firearms as the English.

Selling alcohol to the Indians was perhaps even more danger-ous, certainly to the Indians, but harder to stamp out. The infa-mous Thomas Morton opined that the Indians would "pawne their wits" to buy liquor. Every New England colony passed laws against selling drink to the Indians, but Indians succeeded in ob-taining more drink than was good for them in all those colonies, mostly from English settlers. In time they learned to make their own cider and brandy.

After the Great Migration to Massachusetts Bay in 1630, the pressure of the settlers on Indian lands and hunting grounds steadily increased the tension in ever more complex ways. The first open warfare between Indians and English arose out of friction between rival Indians and rival Europeans, not in Plymouth colony or Massachusetts Bay, but in the more westerly territory that became Connecticut. In 1632 the Dutch, who were beginning to settle the Hudson valley in what would later be New York State, opened a trading post, the House of Hope, near the present site of Hartford, in the Connecticut River valley. The Dutch East India company agent, Jacob Van Cutler, bought the land from the Pe-quot tribe. Not long afterwards a group of entrepreneurs from Ply-mouth claimed prior rights to a location higher up the river that would cut the Dutch out of their access to furs. They did this on the dubious basis of a deed bought from a former sachem of the Pequots who had been expelled by the tribe. English colonists from the Massachusetts Bay Colony were already settling the dis-trict, and John Winthrop Jr. was appointed governor of the Say-brook colony, which was built at the mouth of the river.

A long series of what the English considered Pequot outrages began in 1634 when the Pequots murdered a trading party of Nar-

PEQUOT MASSACRE
*(Illustration courtesy of The Library Company of Philadelphia,
reprinted with permission)*

ragansetts. The conflict escalated during the following two years:
A piratical English sea captain, John Stone, was murdered by Pequots, and in 1636 a more respected English trader, John Oldham,
and eight of his companions were murdered in his boat by Indians
from Block Island. John Endicott, from Massachusetts, led a puni-
tive expedition. His orders were to kill every male member of the
Block Island tribe. Having laid waste to the island he then
marched on the Pequots and inflicted casualties and damage on
them. The Pequots retaliated by raiding Wethersfield, on the Connecticut River. They killed at least nine settlers, possibly thirty,
kidnapped two girls and tortured their captives, as all Algonquian
tribes were sometimes accustomed to do.

So in May 1636, Captain John Mason led ninety men from
Connecticut, and Colonel John Endicott led larger forces from

Massachusetts, to end the Pequot problem forever. Mason's men surprised the Pequots with a dawn attack. Mason himself grabbed a burning brand from a wigwam fire and thrust it into the straw roof. The English soldiers withdrew and shot down the Pequots as they tried to escape. Within half an hour hundreds of Pequots—men, women, and children—were dead. Estimates of their number vary from 400 to 700, but only seven Pequots escaped. Captain Mason gave the glory to God: "this did the Lord judge among the heathen, filling the Place with dead bodies." Captain Underhill agreed: "When a people is grown to such a height of blood and sin against God and man . . . he harrows them, and saws them, and puts them to the sword." Even the gentler William Bradford, who generally walked more humbly with his God, agreed. "It was a frightful sight," he wrote, "to see them thus frying in the fire and the streams of blood quenching the same, and horrible was the stink and scent thereof, but the victory seemed a sweet sacrifice, and they gave the praise thereof to God."[4]

The General Court of Massachusetts decreed June 13, 1636, as a day of thanksgiving. This was one of the earliest, if not the first, thanksgiving celebrations ordered by the authority, not of the church, but of the government. It is ironic that it celebrated a victory won thanks to an act of genocidal violence.

The victory was certainly decisive as far as the Pequots were concerned. The English destroyed them as thoroughly as the Romans erased Carthage from the map. Several score Pequots were executed in cold blood. Pequot lands were given to other tribes. The Pequot people, the Destroyers, were themselves ruthlessly destroyed.

The result of the Pequot war opened up the Connecticut River valley to settlement. Within four years it boasted four thousand English settlers, with another twenty-five hundred in the new colony of New Haven, further west on the Quinnipiac River. The effect was wider than that. "Overnight," writes a leading historian, "the balance of power had shifted from the populous but unorganized natives to the English colonies."[5] The war had also taught the English that they needed to help one another. It led almost directly to the establishment of the New England Confederation between Massachusetts, Plymouth, and Connecticut.

The Pequot war was in a sense not a racial or racist war. In exterminating the Pequots, the English had the cooperation of most of the other Indian tribes of southern New England, in particular the Narragansetts, who joined in shooting down the Pequots as they fled from their burning village. Still, the atmosphere between the English and the Native Americans as a whole had changed. For the next forty years there was constant concern about the intentions of one Indian tribe or another, especially those of the Narragansetts. There were repeated rumors of conspiracy. Many a New England farmer, living on the edge of the forest—far from the inhabited center of his town—worried about the safety of his crops, his roof, and his womenfolk. Yet, from the Pequot war on, it was clear that only a universal conspiracy, capable of recruiting all or almost all of the Native Americans of New England, could threaten English dominance, let alone English survival.

Forty years later, perhaps with a certain inevitability, that is exactly what happened. The causes of the conflagration known as King Philip's War, which did indeed for a few brief months in the 1670s call into question the very survival of New England, were both complex and simple. Complex, because they included an intricate pattern of English immigration, expansion, land speculation, land claims, and land frauds. The New England Indians could have felt with some justification that this pressure threatened to drive them westward into the unloving arms of the Mohawks on the upper Hudson. At the same time daily contacts between the English and the Indians were getting more complicated. Roughly one-fifth of the Native Americans converted to Christianity, whatever that meant exactly. (Edward Winslow gives an amusing example of cultural misunderstanding. He was explaining the principles of Christianity to Hobbamock, Plymouth's Indian neighbor. "I took occasion to tell him of God's works of creation and preservation, of his laws and ordinances, and especially of the Ten Commandments; all of which they harkened unto with great attention, and liked well of; only the seventh commandment they excepted against, thinking there were many inconveniences in it, that a man should be tied to one woman.")

The English victories in King Philip's War, as in the Pequot war forty years earlier, were celebrated with solemn days of humiliation, officially proclaimed by the colonial legislatures. At the same time the clergy issued widespread calls for repentance and a reform of public morals, on the grounds that God could not have allowed the Indians so many victories unless He were displeased with His servants in New England.

By the sort of historical irony that epic poets love, the catastrophe was ignited by Metacom or Philip, the son of Massasoit, the very king of the Wampanoag who had feasted with the Pilgrims at the First Thanksgiving. The trigger was the hanging of three Indians in 1675 after an English jury and an auxiliary Indian jury of "grave and sage men," convicted them of murdering an English-speaking Indian whom they believed to be on the point of revealing Philip's plotting against the English.

A long deterioration of trust had preceded the outbreak of war with much evidence of the growing tension and fears on both sides. War proper began in June 1675 with demonstrations by Indian braves against the village of Swansea, an outpost of Plymouth colony that blocks the neck of land leading to the Wampanoag capital at Mount Hope in Narragansett Bay, Rhode Island. Tradition says it was the English who caused the first fatal casualty, but before long settlers had been murdered in an outlying part of Swansea, and their heads skewered on poles. The war spread to central Massachusetts and to the upper Connecticut valley, and from the Wampanoags to other tribes, the Nipmucks and the Narragansetts, who battled the English in the Great Swamp Fight in December 1675. At one time, Indian raiders, appearing without warning out of the forest, threatened settlements from the Merrimac in the north to within three miles of Plymouth in the south and beyond to the shores of Buzzards Bay. All over southern New England, the smoking ruins of isolated farms, concealing scalped and sometimes mutilated bodies, showed how freely the Indians could move and how ferociously they could strike.

On February 23, the General Court of Massachusetts ordered a solemn day of humiliation, and so did both Connecticut and Plymouth later in the war. Again, there were widespread calls for repentance and a reform of public morals, on the same grounds as before—that God could not have allowed the Indians so many victories if the colonists had been true to His laws.

For a few weeks, there was real fear in New England that the Indians would drive them back, if not into the sea, then at least into a narrow perimeter. "By the late winter and early spring of 1676," writes the historian of King Philip's War, "the Indians were delivering a powerful and devastating attack which conceivably might have driven the English into a relatively restricted area along the coast."[6]

Unknown to the settlers, though, the Indians had shot their bolt. They were hungry, with dwindling supplies of food stashed at the end of long and perilous marches through the forest. Already the English had the advantage in numbers, and could reinforce their forces while the Indians could not hope to replace their casualties. As a last straw, Mohawk raiding parties began to attack the camps where the New England Indians had left their squaws and children. Gradually the English began to receive surrenders, at first of small bands, then mass surrenders, like the 180 Nipmuck braves who gave themselves up at Boston Common in July 1676, bringing the wanted sachem Matoonas and his son with them as proof of their good intentions.

The English had the Nipmucks tie the sachem to a tree and shot him without further ado. It was not easy to decide what to do with the growing numbers of prisoners. Many were summarily executed. A few were settled on land under English supervision. Most were sold into slavery, either overseas or in the Caribbean, or to local white masters.

Under the double pressure of hunger and more effective English warfare, the struggle shrank back from its wider frontiers to the Wampanoag homeland in the rough, marshy southwestern fringe of Plymouth colony. An Indian deserter betrayed to Captain Benjamin Church that King Philip, with a few companions, was revisiting his home village at Mount Hope, near Bristol, Rhode Island.

It was there, in August 1676, that a small mixed force of Plymouth soldiers and Indian warriors surrounded the Wampanoag sachem and his followers. When one English unit drove the surprised Indians towards the blocking force, two Plymouth soldiers, one English, one Indian, saw the sachem running towards them. The Englishman fired but his gun misfired. The Indian fired and the running sachem pitched forward onto his face, dead. It was Philip. When the fight was over, Church went to look at his enemy. He saw "a doleful, great, naked, dirty beast." He ordered the body beheaded and quartered as that of a traitor.

King Philip's War hardened the colonists' attitude to the Indians, and it decided forever that North America would be ruled by the Europeans. Before long, Indian wars had become entangled in the conflict between the English and the French for suzerainty in North America. Three centuries later, attitudes to the Native American people have softened greatly. But the English victory in King Philip's War put an end to the more idealistic visions of mass conversion that William Brewster and William Bradford and their fellows may have cherished as they landed in Provincetown Bay, more than fifty years before the sordid death of Massasoit's son in a muddy ambush, when the Settlers still shared feasts and the hope of enduring friendship with the Wampanoags.

CHAPTER EIGHT

The Colony

Though men have escaped the danger of the Sea,
and that cruel mortality, which swept away so many of
our loving friends and brethren; yet except they purge out
this self-love, a worse mischief is prepared for them.

—Robert Cushman

By 1643 the Pilgrims had perceived that they had not chosen
wisely in establishing the site of their colony at Plymouth, which
was neither a good port nor an area well suited to farming.

—Durand Echevarria

TWO YEARS AFTER THE EVENT REMEMBERED AS THE First Thanksgiving, Plymouth was in trouble again. In fact, the little settlement faced many trials. Its chief financial backer, Thomas Weston, decided to set up a private colony of his own a few miles away. It turned out to be a mess. Then Weston himself showed up unexpectedly. There was trouble with the Indians, and difficulty with others, besides Weston, of the adventurers who had sent the Planters into the wilderness.

The most serious trouble, though, was elemental. There wasn't enough food. Later accounts, saying that they were down to their last five pints of corn, or that they distributed two grains to every settler, are no doubt exaggerated. But in spite of the upbeat reports Edward Winslow and others had sent home, it was nip and tuck whether the colony would survive.

From the start, the Pilgrim venture had two aspects that, if they were not necessarily incompatible, fit awkwardly together. William Brewster, William Bradford, and their friends ventured into the wilderness to gather about them a church that would serve God according to His law as they interpreted it. Thomas Weston and his fellow adventurers in the City of London had more earthly goals. They had invested good money, and they intended to make a return on it.

Very early on, one of their ambitions, to make money from the whales, cod, bass, and other fish that teemed in and around Cape Cod Bay, was ruled out by the Council of New England's grant of a fishing monopoly to Sir Ferdinando Gorges[1] and his allies. The other great staple on which both the Planters—the Pilgrims—and the Adventurers could count was the fur trade, and the Pilgrims did succeed in shipping back many thousands of beaver skins, as well as small quantities of otter and other pelts. But after the first precarious years of the struggle for sheer survival, the history of the colony is to an unedifying degree the story of sordid attempts to cheat the Pilgrims by men who did not share their spiritual motivations: by Thomas Weston, by John Peirce, and later by a member of the Pilgrims' own brotherhood, Isaac Allerton.

William Bradford, generally so restrained in his judgments, revealed what he thought of Weston when he wrote his history, many years after these events. It would be good to remember what the Psalmist said, he reminded his readers: "Put not your trust in princes, nor in the son of man, for there is no help in them." And then he added: "much less in merchants!"

Early in 1622, perhaps doubting whether Plymouth would make it, Weston decided to plant his own colony in New England. He obtained a grant of some 6,000 acres around Massachusetts Bay from the Council for New England and assembled sixty or seventy settlers, all men without families, who were to sail in two ships, *Charity* and *Swan*. But first he sent a small ship, *Sparrow*, to Damariscove Island, off the coast of Maine near Boothbay harbor, a place already well known for many years to European fishermen, to do a reconnaissance towards the Massachusetts country.

Sparrow sent seven men in a shallop, led by a certain Phineas Pratt, down the coast as far as Plymouth. They then explored back up the coast, and found the site they were looking for at Wessagussett, which is now King's Cove in modern Weymouth. After they had gone, Weston's two bigger ships followed. *Charity*, the larger of the two, went on to Virginia, but *Swan* arrived in Plymouth with sixty men. They were a nuisance for the Pilgrims, because food was short and Weston had sent no supplies with them. "That little store of corn we had," wrote Winslow, "was exceedingly wasted by the unjust and dishonest walking of these strangers." To the Pilgrims, they seemed a rough lot. And they were certainly not to be counted among "the godly."

The Wessagussett venture was unpromising from the start, not to say doomed. Unlike *Mayflower*'s passengers, these settlers had no supplies, no leadership, no clear purpose except to make money for Weston, and no idea whatever how to handle the few Indians there. But it made life doubly difficult for the Pilgrims. It depleted their dwindling supplies of food, and it complicated the relations they had been carefully cultivating with the Indians.

Weston's men had put no food aside for the winter, and were soon starving. Some of them made the disastrous mistake of stealing some of the Indians' corn. There is a story that they seriously considered hanging an older, sick man in place of the real thief, who was a hard worker and a useful cobbler. It many or may not be true, but the very fact that it could have been believed reveals the gap between Wessagussett and Plymouth. You have only to imagine William Bradford's likely response if anyone had dared to hint at anything of the kind.

In March 1623, word came to Plymouth that Massasoit, king of the Wampanoag, was near to death. Edward Winslow went to see him and succeeded in curing him. He nursed him carefully. Then he shot a goose at a great range, made goose soup, carefully skimming off the fat, and managed to nurse the sachem back to life. Massasoit was naturally full of praise and gratitude, and summoned Hobbamock, the Indian who lived close to Plymouth, and revealed to him that there was a conspiracy on the part of the Massachusetts Indians to murder all the English, both the men of Wessagussett and the Pilgrims. Hobbamock alerted Winslow, and Winslow in turn told Bradford.

In the meantime one of the leaders of the Wessagussett settlement, Phineas Pratt, managed to make his way to Plymouth to warn the Pilgrims how badly things looked there. It was a nightmare journey. Pratt thought he could hear the howling of wolves, and he had to avoid mud and snow so that the Indians who were following him would lose his track.

Bradford had already received the warning from Massasoit. He decided to send Myles Standish to Wessagussett to see what was happening there. The captain took just eight armed men and sailed up to Wessagussett. He found the Indians in a truculent mood. Two of them in particular, Wituwamet and Pecksuot, were openly threatening. One of them bragged of the sharpness of his knife. It had killed both English and French before, he said, and it would kill some more English soon. He even made the mistake of taunting Captain Shrimp about his short stature.

The next day, April 6, 1623, Standish lured Pecksuot, Wituwamet, and two other Indians into the stockade for a feast. It was an ambush. Five Englishmen were present. At a signal the doors were closed and Standish jumped him, grabbed his knife, and killed Pecksuot. The other Englishmen killed Wituwamet, and Standish cut off his head. Then Standish led some of his men and Weston's, and there was a general fight in the open, which the English won. Standish took Wituwamet's head back to Plymouth and stuck it on a pole as a warning. That, after all, was what they did with traitors' heads in England in those days.

Weston's men had had enough. Most of them decided to give up and set off for Monhegan Island, off the coast of Maine, in the hopes of getting passage back to England on the fishing boats. But Phineas Pratt stayed in Plymouth and some others sailed to Plymouth, where Pratt eventually became one of the leading citizens.

That was the end of the Pilgrims' troubles with Weston's colony, but not the end of Weston. He had not crossed the Atlantic in any of these three ships, but shortly afterwards he took passage on a fishing boat, under a false name and disguised as a blacksmith. In Monhegan or elsewhere in the fishing grounds, he set out in a shallop with a couple of men to see what had happened to his colony. Somewhere between the mouth of the Merrimack River and Piscataqua, on the site of the present Portsmouth, New Hampshire, he was shipwrecked, "for want of skill," Bradford comments uncharitably. He almost drowned, but when he made it to the shore, he was captured by Indians, who helped themselves to everything that had not gone down with the shallop, and even stripped him of his clothes, down to his shirt. He managed to make it to Pisqataqua, borrowed a suit of clothes, and found a passage to Plymouth.

When he got there, having lost none of his bounce and chutzpah as a result of his adventures, the great survivor presented the

Pilgrims with a tricky dilemma. Weston asked if he could borrow some beaver skins. He said he hoped to have a ship with him, well supplied, before long, and when it came he would let the Pilgrims have whatever they needed. They put the case to him bluntly. They wanted to help him, if only in gratitude for his past help. But they were in need themselves, and if they gave him the beaver, there would be a mutiny among the settlers, because the furs were all they had to pay for food. The only answer was to let him have one hundred beaver skins, weighing 170 pounds, but they would have to do it in secret.

So Weston lived to be a nuisance again, a "bitter enemy," says Bradford. He seems to have done pretty well out of his investment in the Pilgrims. One careful estimate[2] is that he and his seventy fellow investors, some big, some small, put up no more than fifteen hundred pounds altogether, including the cost of the *Mayflower* with stores and outfitting for the voyage. They got many times more back in beaver skins and other goods. Weston eventually established himself in Virginia, and made fishing and trading expeditions to the Maine coast. But his was a restless spirit. He was arrested several times in Virginia on one charge or another and moved to Maryland, where he bought new property. He eventually returned to England, deeply in debt, and died in Bristol in 1646.

Weston was by no means the only one of the Adventurers to try to cheat the settlers. In April 1623, a letter arrived from Robert Cushman, who was still acting as the Pilgrims' agent in London, announcing that John Peirce, the holder of the original patent by which the Pilgrims had acquired the right to settle, had tried to sell it to the Company for five hundred pounds. It had cost him just fifty pounds.

That summer was a hard one at Plymouth. In April, the same month when they learned of Peirce's betrayal in London, they planted a crop of corn and a crop of beans. But from the third week in May for six weeks there was hardly a drop of rain. The ears of corn withered and changed color so that they seemed dead. The beans stopped growing, and looked parched "as if they had been scorched before a fire."

The Pilgrims reacted as they had done before in times of trouble, and as they and their descendants would do again and again. Not only did they examine how they stood as between God and their individual consciences, they decided on a collective act of worship to call upon their God to save them as he had done before. They resolved to "humble ourselves before the Lord by fasting and prayer," and the Lord heard their prayer.

When they met in the morning, the sky was clear and the sun was hot. It looked as if the drought would last. They were eight or nine hours in church, or rather, since they had not yet built a church, in the communal building, and before they went home, clouds had gathered. The next morning there came a "soft, sweet and moderate shower of rain," which lasted for fourteen days. "It was hard to say," wrote Winslow in his gratitude, "whether our withered corn or drooping affections were most quickened and revived; such was the bounty and goodness of our God." Shortly afterwards came news that Myles Standish had succeeded in buying supplies from an isolated Scots settler, David Thomson, on what are now called the Isles of Shoals, in Boston Harbor. And then came news that supply ships were on their way from England. As we have seen, it was then that the Pilgrims celebrated what has perhaps a better reason than the feasting of 1621 to be called the First Thanksgiving.

This was not to be the last time that the sheer survival of Plymouth was put at risk by the weather and crop failure. But it was on this occasion that the Pilgrim leadership took a momentous decision. So far they had held the colony's property in common. "From each according to his ability," in the words of the Communist Manifesto, "to each according to his need." Now they decided instead to trust to the invigorating motive of private profit, or rather of each man's determination to survive, and to ensure if he could that his family survived. In Winslow's words, "considering that self-love wherewith every man, in a measure more or less, loveth and preferreth his own good before his neighbour's, and also the base disposition of some drones . . . it was therefore thought best that every man should use the best diligence he could for his own preservation . . . and to prepare his own corn for the year following." They did however allow for a "competent portion" to be set aside for "public officers, fishermen etc."[3]

Bradford reported that dividing up the land between families "had a very good success, for it made all hands very industrious," and increased the amount of corn planted. He added that "the women now went willingly in to the field, and took their little ones with them to set corn." He went on to argue that this experiment, tried by "godly and sober men," proved the vanity "of that conceit of Plato's and other ancients applauded by some of later times: that the taking away of property and bringing in community into a commonwealth would make them happy and flourishing." What he called "community" and others might call "communism," Bradford concluded from experience, did not work. The young and strong resented working for other men's wives and children without recompense. The "aged and graver men" didn't like it either; some of them saw it as indignity and disrespect. As for the wives, to have to work for other men, cooking their meals and washing their clothes, they "deemed it a kind of slavery, nor could many husbands well brook it." One historian[4] noticed that Bradford owned a copy of Richard Knolles's English translation of the French scholar Jean Bodin's *De Republica*, which explicitly attacked Plato. "He understood not," wrote Bodin of Plato, "that by making all things common, a Commonweal must needs perish: for nothing can be public, where nothing is private." Such a commonweal, Bodin added, was also against the law of God and nature "which expressly forbids us to . . . desire anything that another man's is."

The planting of Plymouth, we have seen, had from the beginning a double aspect. To the religious Pilgrims, it offered the enticing prospect of building their own City of God in the wilderness, where none could tell them what to believe or how to worship. To the Merchant Adventurers, even though some of them were sincerely sympathetic to the Puritan religion, it was primarily a business opportunity, an investment that must justify itself by its financial return.

It could be argued that the moment when, pressed by the specter of starvation, the Pilgrims abandoned the goal of an Utopian commonwealth and allowed the profit motive to generate the energy to dig them out of their troubles, was the point in time when the godly and the worldly aspects of the venture changed places. Certainly the Pilgrim leaders continued to be harassed and even cheated by their business partners. Thomas Weston stopped interfering with them after 1623. But at least from the point of view of the godly Bradford, the plantation was to have even worse problems with its own business agent, Isaac Allerton.

When they set out for America, and for the first years after they got there, the Pilgrims turned their back on worldly wealth and success. Their spirit was well expressed in the famous sermon preached by Robert Cushman, he who had negotiated the original deal with Weston and the Adventurers. On December 12, 1621, the first anniversary of the Pilgrims' arrival in Plymouth, Cushman preached on a text from Corinthians (10:24): "Let no man seek his own: But every man another's wealth." "The bane of all these mischiefs which arise among you," he said, "is, that men are too cleaving to themselves and their own matters." And he went on to denounce greed, the "belly-god" in language of true Puritan austerity. "The vain and corrupt heart of man cannot better be resembled than by a belly-god, Host, or Innkeeper, which welcometh his guests with smilings, and salutations, and a thousand welcomes, and rejoiceth greatly to have their company to dice, cards, eat, drink, and be merry, but should not the box be paid, . . . the Epicure's joy would soon be turned into sorrow, and his smiles turned into frowns."[5]

Cushman was quite explicit. It was a good thing to have ventured into the wilderness. But too many of the Pilgrims had done so for the wrong reason, to turn themselves into country gentlemen, another form of self-love. "Men that have taken in hand hither to come," said Cushman, "out of discontentment in regard of their estates in England; and aiming at great matters here, affecting it to be Gentlemen, Landed men, or hoping for Office, Place, Dignity, or fleshy Liberty; let the show be what it will, the substance is naught, and that bird of self-love which was hatched at home, if it be not looked to, will eat out the life of all grace and goodness: and though men have escaped the danger of the Sea, and that cruel mortality, which swept away so many of our loving friends and brethren; yet except they purge out this self-love, a worse mischief is prepared for them."

Isaac Allerton, who succeeded Cushman as the Pilgrims' agent in London, was of a different turn of mind from Cushman. He and his sister Sarah were indeed two of the most respected members of John Robinson's congregation in Leiden, and he was one of the prominent members of *Mayflower*'s company. When Governor John Carver died and Bradford became governor, Allerton became his assistant. After his first wife, Mary, died, he married Elder Brewster's daughter, Fear. (Their daughter, Mary, married Thomas Cushman, who succeeded Brewster as Elder.) Allerton was one of their own, a true member of the inner circle of the Plymouth enterprise. Yet his career illustrates precisely the worldly temptations that Brewster, Bradford, and Robert Cushman were so keen to avoid.

When Cushman died in 1625, Bradford sent Allerton to replace him. Allerton was a man of "uncommon activity, address and enterprise." He understood that the colony was crippled by its debt to Weston and the other London adventurers. In modern terms, Allerton refinanced the debt. He created a new body, the Undertakers, who took over the debt from the adventurers. Allerton arranged for the adventurers to be paid eighteen hundred pounds, "in lawful money of England at the place appointed for the receipts of money on the west side of the Royal Exchange in London." The money was then to be paid back at the rate of two hundred pounds every year.

So far, so good. Allerton was also successful in arranging for the arrival of two boatloads of members of the Leiden church. One group, of thirty-five men, women, and children, left Holland in May and arrived in Plymouth in August 1629; the second group, slightly larger, arrived in late May 1630. The Plymouth community was sad that their beloved pastor, John Robinson, could not be with the newcomers. But Bradford saw the gathering of the church that had been separated for almost a decade as "the special work and hand of God."

He and his friends were less pleased when Allerton explained that the operation would cost five hundred pounds, and that this would only cover their trip from Holland as far as Salem, where they landed in America, and not their onward passage to Plymouth. Bradford's eyebrows rose when Allerton appeared in Plymouth with goods which he proceeded to sell to the people of Plymouth on his own account. They rose even further when Allerton appeared with none other than the Lord of Misrule from Merrymount, Thomas Morton, whom Bradford thought he had safely dispatched back to England. Things went seriously wrong, however, when Bradford and his friends in Plymouth learned from London that their own agent, Allerton, without telling them, had committed them to a fur trading venture at Penobscot, near the present town of Castine, Maine, and had sent out one Edward Ashley, a "profane young man," with a good supply of trade goods, more than Allerton's own clients in Plymouth could boast.

Things went from bad to worse. Ashley was caught selling powder and shot to the Indians. He was in serious trouble, because King Charles I in London had issued a proclamation forbidding "the furnishing of the Natives . . . with Weapons and Habiliments of Warre." (Ashley was also "profane" enough to have "committed uncleanness with Indian women," as Bradford put it.) Bradford was able to rescue a thousand pounds' weight of beaver because he had had the foresight to make Ashley sign a bond that he would not sell arms to the Indians. But Ashley was taken back to England as a prisoner and locked up in the Fleet jail. He managed to talk his way out and went on a trading mission to Russia, but was drowned at sea on his way home.

Bradford was particularly annoyed by Allerton's behavior in the matter of a ship called, perhaps rather inappropriately, *White Angel*, in which Allerton had arrived on the Maine coast. Allerton's friend, the Undertaker James Sherley, a London goldsmith and banker who thought nothing of charging 30 percent and even higher rates of interest on his loans to the Pilgrims, wrote explaining that the ship was to be used both for trading and for fishing. Bradford was angry to discover that *White Angel*, which was supposed to be used for fishing on the Plymouth account, was in fact used to carry freight at high rates per ton for the Puritans, who were now emigrating in their thousands to Massachusetts Bay. Worse, it turned out that Allerton and Sherley had met and dined at a London tavern with a factor to discuss selling *White Angel* at Oporto, in Portugal, for their own profit.

Bradford took seriously the duty of Christian charity, and he sought to deal with Allerton "with pity and compassion." He said with the apostle Timothy that "they that will be rich will fall into many snares and temptations," for "the love of money is the root of all evil." He hoped therefore that Allerton would find mercy by repentance for the wrongs he had done "this poor plantation."

Certainly the plantation was the poorer for its dealings with Allerton. It was in 1627 that he transferred the colony's debt to the Undertakers. In 1628, when things had had time to be sorted out, Plymouth's debt stood at some four hundred pounds. When Bradford and his fellow leaders were presented with Allerton's account just over two years later, it was a mess. Some items were charged twice. At one point Allerton blotted and overwrote some words to conceal what he was up to. He "screwed up his poor old father-in-law's account," that is William Brewster's, to more than two hundred pounds, and didn't seem to give the colony fair credit for the large quantities of valuable beaver fur they had shipped over. The total debt stood at the unconvincingly precise figure of £4,770 19 s. 2d., plus another £1,000 for "purchases unpaid." For such supplies, Allerton's friend Sherley charged 50 percent interest. In a word, Plymouth's affairs had been for more than two years in the hands of a crook. He and his accomplices had fleeced them pitilessly.

DISTRESSING AS IT WAS FOR THE PILGRIMS—MEN AND women who had deliberately put worldly wealth behind godliness in their scale of values—to be cheated financially as they were by Weston, John Peirce, and Isaac Allerton, one of their own, it was not these financial setbacks that changed Plymouth's prospects, so much as the success of the Massachusetts Bay plantation, only a few miles up the coast.

After the accession of Charles I in 1625, it was clear that church policy in England threatened to be even more hostile to the godly than it had been under James I. The party led by Archbishop William Laud—known as the Arminians, though their theology was only tenuously related to the beliefs of that Arminius against whom John Robinson had debated in Leiden—intended to enforce obedience to their views, which the more extreme Protestants regarded as little better than Roman Catholicism. Actual persecution could not be ruled out, and in fact a few years after the Massachusetts Puritans left William Prynne was whipped and had his ears cut off as a judicial punishment for attacking the immorality of the theater. The bishops punished people, though not in such a brutal manner, for such liturgical offences as not kneeling in prayer at the prescribed moments.

For some time members of the Protestant persuasion had been thinking about emigrating. It was in 1628, after Charles I had dissolved Parliament and embarked on a period of "personal rule," that a wealthy and powerful group of Puritans, godly folk, that is, but who had decided not to break publicly with the Church of England, decided to follow the Pilgrims' example and emigrate to North America. They were able to do so with far stronger resources and in far greater numbers than the Plymouth colony.

As long ago as 1613 a devastating fire had burned much of the town of Dorchester, county town of Dorset in southwestern England. The rector of Holy Trinity church there, an evangelical Calvinist called the Reverend John White, saw the fire as a sign from heaven that Dorchester must be cleansed from sin. He conceived of the Dorchester Company to raise money for emigration. In 1623 White and his company succeeded in receiving a patent from the Council for New England, itself a reorganization of the old Virginia Company. This was the company associated with Sir Ferdinando Gorges, and Robert Rich, earl of Warwick, one of the wealthiest noblemen in England, and a staunch Puritan, was a member of it.

John White, though a Calvinist, was also a loyal Anglican. He saw his colony as a bulwark both against the spread of Catholic power, and also against the separatist impulse that had created Plymouth. The Dorchester Company established a number of settlements on the New England coast, including the one founded by Roger Conant, which in 1625 moved from Cape Ann to Naumkeag, later christened Salem. But these were fragile ventures. More capital would be needed. John White and his friends went to contacts in the City of London and brought in as investors both rich merchants and Puritan gentlemen such as Sir Richard Saltonstall and John Winthrop of Groton. Once again, the support for a colony in North America was to come, partly from the search for religious freedom, and partly from the profit motive.

On March 4, 1629, a royal charter was granted to the Massachusetts Bay Company. Its governor was John Endecott, and a number of prominent men agreed to settle overseas, including the Reverend Francis Higginson, Samuel Skelton, and Francis Bright. (It is remarkable how many names later famous in New England history were in it from the beginning—Conant, Endecott, Higginson, Winthrop, and Saltonstall.) The investors, who decided not to emigrate for the time being, included many of the Puritan faction in the high aristocracy of Eastern England, from Essex north to Lincolnshire, where Protestant faith was most deeply implanted. They included the wealthy earl of Warwick, and his Rich family, from Essex, and the earl of Lincoln and his Fiennes-Clinton family from Lincolnshire, and many other gentry families, among them Pelhams and Waldegraves. These grandees, in that still-feudal society, brought along with them dependents, stewards like Thomas Dudley, a future governor of Massachusetts, and clergy such as John Cotton, the forefather of a great clan of New England divines. And among them they included one man with connections both in the legal world of London and among the Protestant divines of Essex, John Winthrop, who was ready to cross the seas himself.

The Massachusetts Bay colony grew far more quickly than Plymouth. In 1629, there were three hundred settlers at Salem, and another one hundred at Charlestown, across the river from where

Boston was to stand. In 1630 the Narragansett Indians made a determined effort to destroy the English, even apparently those at Plymouth. The Salem settlers scared the Indians away by firing their cannon. It was soon too late for the Indians to hope to drive the English into the sea. In the first year seventeen ships brought over one thousand settlers to the Massachusetts Bay Colony. By 1632 the population had doubled to two thousand, and by 1634 it had doubled again. By 1640, after ten years, the English population of Massachusetts had reached twelve thousand, and the colony had been divided into four counties. (Interestingly they were given, and have retained, the names of four counties in the East of Old England: Essex, Suffolk, Norfolk, and Middlesex.) By the same time, the English population of New England as a whole was well past twenty thousand, while the native population was declining rapidly due to another epidemic in 1633–34 and also to the "Pequot War" of 1636–37.

Plymouth was also becoming embroiled in conflicts, minor and not so minor, with its neighbors, the new colonies. There was the case of John Stone, an English pirate with a scandalous reputation: He was said to have been reduced to cannibalism after a shipwreck. He attempted to seize a Plymouth ship in the harbor of New Amsterdam. When he sailed north to Boston, the Plymouth authorities sent Myles Standish to arrest him. John Winthrop preferred to send him to England to be tried there. To avoid conflict with Plymouth, Winthrop released Stone, who rewarded his leniency by getting drunk and ending up in bed with a married Massachusetts lady. When he was arrested he called one of the magistrates a "just ass."

More serious was the Hocking affair. In the effort to repay the debts accumulated by Allerton and increased by the rates of interest demanded by Sherley and other London bankers, Plymouth was relying heavily on fishing on what is now the coast of Maine. The Plymouth fishery was on the Kennebec River east of Casco Bay. A powerful group of English Puritan noblemen and gentlemen, including Lord Saye and Sele and Lord Brooke (founders of Saybrook, Connecticut) bought land on the Piscataqua, near what is now Portsmouth, New Hampshire. In 1634 one of the fishermen they employed, John Hocking, or Hockin, appeared on what the Plymouth fishermen regarded as their water on the Kennebec. John Howland, a prominent Pilgrim, challenged Hocking. An altercation, then an affray followed, in which Hocking and Plymouth's Moses Talbot were both shot dead. Here was an affair with the potential for serious trouble. Lords Saye and Brooke might well have carried the quarrel back to the English courts, with the possibility of intervention from London. As it was, tempers were skillfully calmed by John Winthrop and his deputy, Thomas Dudley.[6]

These and other frictions between the colonies, especially over land and boundaries, and above all the danger from Indian conspiracies and uprisings, brought home by the Pequot war, motivated Massachusetts to press for some kind of structured relationship between the colonies. New England was divided between Plymouth, Massachusetts, Rhode Island (settled in the Narragansett country by Roger Williams in 1636), and the several colonies that would become Connecticut. By 1643 all difficulties and jealousies had been overcome and the New England Confederation had come into existence, with Plymouth, Massachusetts, and Connecticut, but not Rhode Island, as members. (At first there were four colony members, as Saybrook and New Haven had not yet merged to become Connecticut.) Each of the three colonies sent two commissioners who met by rotation in Plymouth, Boston, and Hartford, but for action five out of the six votes were required, so that in effect each of the three members had a veto. It was in the main, therefore, a "talking shop," a place for discussion and consultation. Only occasionally, as in the crisis of King Philip's War in the 1670s, did it become an effective political and indeed military entity.

By 1640, if not before, Plymouth was becoming a backwater. It was quickly passed in population not only by Massachusetts, but by Connecticut, too, which by the 1670s had twice the population of Plymouth. It was cut off from expansion inland into river valleys and arable land by Massachusetts and Rhode Island. Its location at the bottom of Cape Cod Bay meant that Boston and also Salem had much superior trading opportunities. "By 1643," writes one distinguished local historian, "the Pilgrims had perceived that they had not chosen wisely in establishing the seat of their colony at Plymouth, which was neither a good port, nor an area well suited for farming."[7] Though the immediate surroundings of Plymouth were fertile, inland the land was not suitable for farming. As for the harbor, not only was the entrance a tortuous passage through treacherous sandbanks, but freight had to be transshipped into lighters before it could be landed.

Ironically, it was the creation and rapid growth of Massachusetts Bay that saved Plymouth from the financial dangers that had so much preoccupied its leaders as they struggled to free themselves from the tentacles of first the London Adventurers, then Allerton and the Undertakers. Plymouth and its satellite towns found a market in Boston and the other Bay settlements for their produce. "Corn and cattle rose to a great price," wrote William Bradford, "by which many were much enriched and commodities grew plentiful."[8] But this, too, threatened the character of Plymouth as the Pilgrims had envisioned it.

Plymouth had started as one town, with one church. Within half a generation it had become the capital of an expanded colony. The church and village of Scituate were founded in 1636, Duxbury in 1637, Sandwich, Barnstable, Yarmouth, and Taunton by 1639, and Marshfield in 1641. Other settlements to the west as far as Narragansett Bay, Swansea, and Rehoboth, came into existence at about the same time.

By 1644 Plymouth was even thinking officially of abandoning the Rock (if indeed it had yet appeared) and the Town Brook and moving bodily to a new site. A committee of seven leading citizens was authorized to examine a site near Nauset, one of four sites that had been reserved for purchase by the Old Comers or original settlers in 1640, and to buy land from the Indians. It duly reported back that the site was not big enough to support the population of Plymouth. It had no harbor, and was too remote. Nevertheless they liked the look of it for themselves, and proceeded to buy the land from the sachem of Manamoyick and from George, the sachem of the Nausets. This became the town of Eastham. The land north of George's boundary, now Wellfleet, Massachusetts, was then known as Billingsgate, after the famous London fish market, because the Pilgrims simply could not believe the abundance of fish and seafood—cod, bass, herring, eels, mussels, and much else—in the creeks and ponds of what is now Wellfleet Bay.

Plymouth made one very special contribution to American civilization: the first code of law on American soil. As early as 1623 the colony recorded the decisions of its court, and from 1636 a committee of the General Court composed a legal code. It has been called a "rudimentary bill of rights," insofar as it adapts the famous guarantee in Magna Carta by providing that "no person . . . shall be endamaged in respect of life, limb, liberty, good name or estate . . . but by virtue of some express law of the General Court of this Colony, the known law of God, or the good and equitable laws of our Nation."[9] The colony held elections annually to choose the governor, his seven assistants, and other officers. Any man, whether or not he was a Freeman of the colony, could vote, provided he had taken an oath of allegiance to Plymouth, was the head of a household, and was a settled resident. Only Freemen, however, could be elected to office. Only eight offences were punishable by the death penalty, as against hundreds in England at the time. There was a great controversy, reported by Bradford in great detail in his book, about whether sodomy was a capital crime. (It arose out of a case of bestiality committed by a certain Granger, who was hanged for interfering with a mare and various other creatures, all of which were executed like him.) Three learned ministers were asked to decide, on the basis of Old Testament authority, not only this question, but also whether torture was permissible to get a confession of sodomy, and how many witnesses would be needed to convict. In fact in Plymouth only those convicted of murder or sodomy were ever executed. Adulterers, however, could be made to wear the scarlet letter A on their clothing. In general, contrary to the impression left by Nathaniel Hawthorne and other accounts of the Salem witch panic, the laws of Plymouth were relatively lenient by the standards of the time. No woman was ever charged with witchcraft in Plymouth.

The expansion of Plymouth brought a modest prosperity and created beautiful communities that worked hard for their living until they were swept up in the tourist wave and the writers and artists' colonies of the twentieth century. But this was not what William Bradford and the Pilgrims had in mind when they came from Leiden. Their followers went out to look for land to till and for their cattle. "By which means," wrote Bradford sadly, "they were scattered all over the Bay quickly and the town in which they lived compactly till now was left very thin and in a short time almost desolate."

That implied something even more disastrous for Bradford and for those who shared his nostalgia for the original dream. Even when some of the Pilgrims, including Myles Standish and John Alden, migrated no farther than to Duxbury, the first settlement north of Plymouth harbor, it was too far to get to church. In winter it was not always safe to sail there in a shallop, and ten miles across country was a weary way to church. First Duxbury, then Marshfield, where Edward Winslow had built himself a fine home, then Eastham established churches of their own. Bradford and the other Old Comers had no objection to new churches coming into existence. They were pleased that the church in Massachusetts was in the hands of friends like John Cotton, who had helped them when they were trying to escape to Holland in 1608.

They saw the dispersal of their own church, however, as a tragedy. By the time Plymouth folk had migrated to settlements close to Narragansett Bay or halfway up Cape Cod, the vision of a gathered church was shattered. Plymouth was becoming just another part of Puritan New England, and in 1691 it was formally annexed and became part of Massachusetts.

One survivor of *Mayflower*'s journey lived until after the annexation. Mary Cushman, daughter of Isaac Allerton, died in 1699, aged eighty-three. The core members of the Plymouth adventure were disappearing through migration or death long before that. William Brewster, who had been born in 1567, died in 1644. Edward Winslow left for England in 1646 and never came back. He was sent by Oliver Cromwell as commissioner to the British settlements in the West Indies, and died on the way there in 1655. Myles Standish died in 1656, and William Bradford in 1657.

"And thus," Bradford had written sadly in 1650, "was this poor church left, like an ancient mother grown old and forsaken of her children, though not in their affections yet in regard of their bodily presence and personal helpfulness; her ancient members being most of them worn away by death, and these of later time being like children translated into other families, and she a widow left only to trust in God. Thus, she that had made many rich became herself poor."[10]

CHAPTER NINE

Fasts and Thanksgivings

If it has kinship with anything in the past,
it is to the Harvest Home of England.

—WILLIAM DeLoss LOVE

THE LATE-NINETEENTH-CENTURY CONNECTICUT MINISTER and scholar William DeLoss Love wrote a meticulous history of *Fasts and Thanksgivings in New England*. Right at the end, as an apparent afterthought, he added an appendix. His excitement shows through. He had found, he thought, the very first Thanksgiving of the Pilgrims in America.

The family Bible of *Mayflower* Pilgrim, William White—Love reported—had been discovered. It was a Breeches Bible[1] of 1588, and it had supposedly passed to one S. W. Cowles, a citizen of Hartford, Connecticut. It had perhaps been left by White's widow, Susanna, née Winslow, to none other than William Brewster, and had also perhaps belonged to John Howland, the leading Pilgrim who was saved from drowning on *Mayflower*'s voyage by luckily catching a rope as he was being washed overboard.

According to Love, the Bible contained the following (poorly spelled) inscription. "William White Maried on ye 3d day of March 1620 to Susannah Tilly. Peregrine Whitee Born on Boared ye Mayflower in Cape Cod harber. Sonne born to Susanna Whtee December 19 1620 yt Six-o-clock morning. Next day we met for prayer and thanksgiving."

Love concluded triumphantly that he had found the first thanksgiving. It happened on December 20, 1620, just ten days after the reconnaissance party landed on Clark's Island in Plymouth Bay.

It is not surprising that the Pilgrims gave thanks to God for their deliverance. Indeed William Bradford records that, the morning after they first landed on Clark's Island, a "fair, sunshining day, and they found themselves on an island secure from the Indians," they "gave thanks to God for His mercies in their manifold deliverances." That was their way.

William White's family Bible, however, turned out to be not quite what it seemed to the Reverend Love, as came to light in a most unexpected way. About 1990, the staff of the Harry Ransom Center at the University of Texas in Austin decided to move a small book truck full of the library's treasures, which had stood for some years near the reference desk. There is a hint that it seemed a little unsophisticated for what has become one of the world's leading collections of literary rarities. As the items were being put away, one of them caught the eye of a reference librarian. It claimed to be a Bible that had reached America on *Mayflower*. It was, in fact, a Breeches Bible, that is, a Geneva Bible, the preferred Bible of Elizabethan Puritans.

The librarian was professionally skeptical. The book not only recorded births, deaths, and arrivals in New England, including the birth of Peregrine White, son of the owner, and the first European child born in New England. It was quaintly and copiously illustrated, with pen-and-ink drawings of Indians with bows and arrows and the like in the margins. The librarian recruited the help of John B. Thomas III, chief of rare book cataloging at the Ransom Center.[2]

Mr. Thomas and his colleague easily established that the book had been unearthed by a bookseller in Manchester, Connecticut, Charles M. Taintor, and that it had been bought from him for twelve dollars by S. W. Cowles. It was inherited from him by a Mrs. S. W. Cowles, presumably his widow or daughter-in-law. It was described in a newspaper article in Los Angeles in 1912, and was then bought by Miriam Lutcher Stark of Orange, Texas, who gave it to the Ransom Center in the late 1920s. The only information about its earlier history was that it had apparently been in England during part of the eighteenth century.

After carefully checking the annotations in the Bible against the known information about the Pilgrims and Plymouth, Thomas could find no obvious howlers that might have proved that it was a fraud. However, there was one peculiarity. The Bible was bound up with a substantial fragment of a Book of Common Prayer, the Church of England's official service book. That in itself was curious, if not suspicious. Why, after all, would a Separatist, emigrating to New England to free himself from the regulation of the Church of England, want to bind up with his Geneva Bible that Church's official Book of Common Prayer?

Thomas spent a good deal of time and effort checking and rechecking the inscriptions. Eventually he noticed something else. The pages from the Book of Common Prayer were in quarto, printed in black letter type, two columns to a page. The pages were gathered, or bound, in signatures of eight, except for signature B, which had eleven leaves. With growing curiosity, Thomas counted and recounted the pages: There were indeed eleven of them, which is of course impossible in normal binding. The explanation was that, while the first eight leaves of signature B were from one edition of the prayer book, the additional three leaves came from a different quarto edition of the prayer book. Pages from two different editions of the Book of Common Prayer had been bound up together.

The only hope of identifying which editions these pages came from lay in checking what are known as the "state prayers," the places where the prayer book calls on God to bless the head of the Church of England, that is, the reigning king or queen. The prayers in the second fragment, the three pages, called, as they should have done, for divine blessing on Queen Elizabeth. That fit with the 1588 date of the Bible. But the first fragment, too, had state prayers. And Thomas found to his astonishment, that these were not for Queen Elizabeth, or for James I, who was on the throne when the Pilgrims sailed for America, but for James's son, King Charles I, who succeeded to the throne in 1625, for his queen, Henrietta Maria, whom he married in 1628, and for their child, Prince Charles, later Charles II, who was not born until 1630. Further research established that, though the inscriptions in the book included "William White his booke 1619" and "This booke to Mr. William Brewster his booke from Susana White 1623," the prayer book bound up with it was in the edition of 1634. Beyond any reasonable doubt, the University of Texas's *Mayflower* Bible was not what it purported to be. As Mr. Thomas put it to the author, "The proof was in the examination of the book itself." It didn't matter what the inscriptions in the book were. "If any [were] written on something that went through the press in the 1630s, and those notes pretend to be written in the 1620s at the latest, then the artefact is a fake."

MOST CULTURES AND RELIGIONS AROUND THE WORLD HAVE celebrated the successful bringing in of the harvest for the year with some sort of religious ceremony of thanks to their God or gods. This was true of ancient Greece and Italy, of China and the Korean peninsula, of the Indian subcontinent, and ancient Egypt. The Greek Demeter and the Latin Ceres were goddesses of the harvest, and their festivals were harvest rituals. The Jewish Sukkoth, the "feast of tabernacles," was also Hag ha Asif, the "feast of ingathering," or harvest.[3] The Ga people of northern Ghana, many of whom have moved to the capital, Accra, observe the festival of Homowo, "hooting at hunger," in late summer. The Japanese celebrate the rice harvest with rituals of great sanctity; indeed the Japanese emperor himself was originally the shaman who conducted the harvest ceremony. Native American peoples–among them the Creek, Cherokee, Seminole, and Iroquois, as well as many other tribes–celebrate an elaborate Green Corn ceremony when the corn is ready to harvest.

Even before their conversion to Christianity, the various peoples of the British Isles, too, celebrated the successful end of the harvest every year. The Celts in Great Britain, before the arrival of the English, and in Ireland honored Lugh, the god of light, with the festivals of Lughnasad (pronounced Lunasa). The Germanic peoples, too—Angles, Saxons, and Jutes—who settled in England and merged to form the English people, ancestors of the Pilgrims, had their own harvest festival in the autumn, which they called Lammastide, or "the time of the loaf." They plaited wheat or barley stalks into "corn dollies," goddesses of the harvest, made from the first and the last of the crop to be reaped. Sometimes they sacrificed an animal, often a hare caught in the crop as it was diminished by the reapers as they worked inwards from the edge of the field. They decorated the horse that pulled in the last load. Harvest home was celebrated with feasting.

The farmer and his laborers celebrated the death and rebirth of what in Christian times became John Barleycorn, the spirit of the harvest, with copious draughts of beer. "John," of course, is a Hebrew, Greek and Christian name, so John Barleycorn is a reminder of the way in which, before the Reformation, these ancient folk traditions were taken over by the Christian church, no doubt tamed of some of their pagan boisterousness, and brought into harmony with the feast days of the Christian year.

After the Reformation, when Protestants saw the Church's medieval festivals as survivals of Romish superstition, harvest festivals declined. But in 1843 the Reverend Stephen Hawker, poet and Anglican parson of a remote Cornish parish, whose wild parishioners included smugglers and wreckers who lured passing ships on to the rocks with false lights, revived the custom of holding harvest festivals in church. It was not long before the harvest festival became one of the favorite festivals of the church year. To this day, in country districts in England, children bring fruit and vegetables, as well as sheaves of corn, to decorate the church, and the congregation sing harvest home hymns, among them a song first heard in a North German farmhouse and written down by Matthias Claudius in the eighteenth century:

> We plough the fields, and scatter the good seed on the land,
> but it is fed and watered by God's almighty hand:
> he sends the snow in winter, the warmth to swell the grain,
> the breezes, and the sunshine, and soft, refreshing rain.

As part of their rebellion against Rome and its traditions, the Pilgrims, like other Protestants in sixteenth- and seventeenth-century England, did not keep Christmas, Good Friday, or even Easter, let alone the saints' days and the other high days of the Christian year. As we have seen, they kept only three days as special: the Lord's day (Sunday) every week; days of prayer and humiliation, when the wickedness of the people had brought God's wrath upon them, or when some especially dangerous decision needed to be taken such as the decision to embark at Delfshaven for the New World; and days of thanksgiving when God's mercy had been vouchsafed in delivering his people from war, famine, pestilence, or some other great peril. A fast day, of course, can turn into a feast day, rather as good Muslims, when the fasting of Ramadan ends, allow themselves to eat, though not to drink, and to be merry. So, though fasts and thanksgivings are very different, inspired as they are by very different religious feelings, in practice it is not always easy for the historian to tell them apart.

There have been in the course of American history festivals, whether of fasting or thanksgiving, appointed by a church or group of churches, and others set by the secular authority. In part therefore the history of Thanksgiving is the transition from religious services, set by the churches to thank God for his kindness and mercy, or to pray for his help, and secular celebrations, established first by royal governors, and then by the States, severally or together, as public commemorations. Finally, there is the transition between the separate thanksgiving days appointed by the states, and the national Thanksgiving holiday, called for by presidential proclamation by Abraham Lincoln and his successors in the White House. So the history of Thanksgiving is a thread running through the wider history of the United States since the earliest colonial origins, a national interpretation of an almost universal human custom that has many things to say about the American experience and the American philosophy. The enthusiasm with which Americans have embraced a holiday that reflects their gratitude at being Americans says a lot about the quality of American patriotism.

THE SEPARATISTS IN HOLLAND MAY OR MAY NOT HAVE kept the great Christian festivals. Their own tradition would have discouraged them from doing so, but the Dutch Protestants who surrounded them celebrated Christmas and Easter. William of Orange, the great leader of the Dutch Protestant rebellion against Catholic rule, himself kept the feasts of Christmas, Easter, and Whitsuntide (Pentecost). We do know that both Henry Ainsworth, of the Old Church in Amsterdam, and the Pilgrims own beloved pastor, John Robinson, favored fasting as an aid to prayer, and on three separate occasions, as the Pilgrim community in Leiden debated whether or not to emigrate, its members solemnly fasted and prayed together. The first time was in the fall of 1617. The second was in late 1619, and the third was at the very moment of their departure for Delfshaven, when Robinson preached on his text from Ezra: "At the river, by Ahava, I proclaimed a fast."

In America, too, the Pilgrim church of Plymouth kept both days of fasting and humiliation, and days of thanksgiving, almost from the beginning, and so too did the colonies of Massachusetts Bay and Connecticut in due course.

In July 1623, there were examples both of a fast day and of a thanksgiving.[4] On July 16, as we have seen, there was a day of prayer and fasting occasioned by the apparent failure of the harvest, and on July 30 there was a day of thanksgiving for the coming of the rain and also for the arrival of Myles Standish with supplies from the Maine coast, and for news that the supply ship due from England was not, as they had feared, lost. "So that having these many signs of God's favor and acceptation," wrote Winslow,[5] "we thought it would be great ingratitude, if secretly we should smother up the same, or content ourselves with private thanksgiving for that which by private prayer could not be obtained.[6] And therefore another solemn day was set apart and appointed for that end; wherein we returned glory, honor, and praise, with all thankfulness, to our good God, which dealt so graciously with us ..."

The Reverend William Love compiled a voluminous calendar of both days of fasting and humiliation and days of thanksgiving for a variety of reasons, starting from the earliest days of both the

Plymouth and Massachusetts Bay colonies. July 20, 1629, was held as a solemn day of humiliation for the choice of a pastor and a teacher for the church at Plymouth. Thanksgivings were held for the arrival of ships in 1631, twice in 1632, and again twice in 1633. As early as 1630, Plymouth actually kept a fast day in sympathy with the Bay colony. When the Reverend John Lothrop conducted a fast at Scituate, with a suggestion that the feasting after the fast was used to dispense charity to the less well off members of the community, it was, according to Love, the earliest known example in the history of Plymouth of feasting in connection with a thanksgiving day.

In the 1630s the loyal Protestants of Plymouth and Massachusetts duly celebrated the victories of the Protestant champion, King Gustavus Adolphus of Sweden, in the Thirty Years War. It may seem strange to those brought up to think of the Pilgrims as men and women turning their backs on the religious conflicts of Europe, but the Pilgrims and the Puritans followed events in Germany closely. On October 12, 1637, for example, they called for a "day of public thanksgiving to God for his great mercies in subduing the Pequots, bringing the soldiers in safety . . . and good news from Germany." The good news was perhaps either the news of victories by the Swedish army under another general, Baner, or possibly the success of the Dutch army, joined by English and French troops, in the siege of Breda.

During the middle years of the seventeenth century the civil authorities also answered the right to call for days of fasting or thanksgiving. On July 23, 1640, for example, as the crisis that was to break out in the Civil War developed in England, the authorities in Massachusetts proclaimed a fast day because Charles I had dissolved the Short Parliament. On several subsequent occasions in the English Civil War Massachusetts ordered fasts in sympathy with the English Parliament, whereas in 1644, royalist Virginia fasted on Good Friday for "the good success of the king."

The colonies also ordered fasts for troubles nearer home. The seventeenth-century preachers of New England were inclined to blame natural disasters, including droughts, floods, hailstorms, high winds, and recurrent visitations of the seventeen-year locust, as well as plagues, influenza, and smallpox epidemics, on "degenerate ways," though Increase Mather warned that "praying without reforming would not do."

The victorious end of King Philip's War called for thanksgiving, and that meant feasting as well as fasting. On October 23, 1676, the General Court of Connecticut proclaimed "a day of publique Thanksgiving" for the following week to thank God for "appearing so gloriously . . . in subduing of our enemies." Two days later the General Court of Massachusetts followed suit, thanking God that "of those several tribes and parties that have risen up against us . . . there now scarcely remaynes a name or family of them in their former habitations but are either slayne, captivated or fled into the remote parts of the wilderness." On August 12, even before the news of King Philip's death, the Governor of Plymouth gave the order for "publick Thanksgiving," and the next Thursday the people of Plymouth duly climbed to the summit of Burial Hill, carrying swords and muskets as well as their Ainsworth prayer books. Shortly after worship ended, Church's company marched up with Philip's gory head.

In spite of the victory over the Indians, the New England divines of the 1670s, led by Increase Mather, were convinced that fasts were necessary if their congregations were not to lapse into sin. They specifically called for fasts to renew the covenant between their churches and God; these were called "Reformation fasts." On May 9, 1676, Mather preached an "earnest exhortation" on the need for a "solemn renewal of the Covenant with God" and three years later he was asking "what are ye evils that have provoked the Lord to bring his Judgments on New England," and "what is to be done that so these evils may be reformed?"

Authority for ordering fasts was largely vested in the churches until Sir Edmund Andros arrived from New York to be governor of Massachusetts in 1686, when he asserted that proclaiming days of thanksgiving was his right. Under Anglican influence there was a revival of Christmas, Easter, and even saints' days. It was too much when Andros wanted January 30 to be kept as a day of fasting and humiliation to commemorate the beheading of Charles I in 1649. He was removed after the overthrow of James II in 1688 by the Protestant William of Orange, husband of James' sister.

By the end of the seventeenth century, in spite of the attempt on the part of the civil authorities to take control of these days of fasting and feasting from the churches, both had become firmly settled as a regular part of the religious life of New England churches. In Plymouth, the custom of celebrating a thanksgiving with a feast was established from about the middle of the century, though it was not until 1668 that this was explicitly connected with "the fruits of the earth." In Connecticut, the idea of a harvest thanksgiving was accepted from 1649 and ordered by the civil authority annually. There were no regular fast or thanksgiving days in Massachusetts, but an autumn thanksgiving day was usual after about 1660. There were even fasts to invoke the Lord's help against witchcraft in the 1690s.

During the later colonial period, this pattern was maintained. There were special days of fasting to pray for the colonies and their defenders in times of war, between 1688 and 1713, and again at the time of King George's War in the early 1740s, and the French and Indian War in the late 1750s. At the same time days of fast and humiliation marked the great earthquake that shook the East Coast from Kennebec to Philadelphia. Cotton Mather rang the bell of the Old North Church in Boston and preached on a text from Micah: "The Glorious God has roared out of Zion, we have the last night herd the terrible Roaring." In 1749 a public fast was proclaimed for "the severest drought in this country, as has ever been known in the memory of ye oldest persons among us."

Thanksgiving days were intensely politicized in the Revolution, as can be imagined. In 1765 the royal governor of Massachusetts named December 5 as a day to thank God for the birth of a royal child, but that same month Connecticut named a fast day because of "dark aspects of Divine Providence with regard to their most dear and inalienable rights and privileges." In 1774, after the Boston port bill, fasts were announced in Rhode Island, New Hampshire, Massachusetts, and Connecticut, but when the Provincial Assembly petitioned him to set aside a special day for prayer and fasting because of the unsettled times, Governor Thomas Gage of Massachusetts did not even bother to reply. "The request," he said, "was only to give an opportunity for sedition to flow from the pulpit." He was right.

A committee of eminent divines, led by John Winthrop of Harvard, drafted for John Hancock's signature a notably tactful proclamation for the first Provincial Congress in October 1774.

> From a consideration of the continuance of the Gospel among us, and the smiles of Divine Providence upon us with the regard to the seasons of the year, and the general health which has been enjoyed; and in particular from a consideration of the Union which so remarkably prevails not only in this province, but through this continent at this alarming crisis it is RESOLVED . . . that it is highly proper that a day of PUBLIC THANKSGIVING should be observed.

Massachusetts would pray, the Provincial Congress suggested, that

> Harmony and Union . . . be restored between Great-Britain and these Colonies, that we may again rejoice in the Smiles of our Sovereign and the Possession of those Privileges which have been transmitted to us, and have the hopeful

Prospect that they shall be handed down intire to Posterity, under the Protestant Succession in the illustrious House of Hanover.

Four years later, the world had been turned upside down. The Americans had decided they could do without the smiles of George III, and that they would fight for their own privileges. Now General Washington, in the tented field, was calling on his army to thank another monarch for his benevolence.

The glorious intelligence being announced, that Congress have negotiated a treaty of alliance with the Court of France, General Washington has issued the following orders for the army to celebrate the momentous event:

"Head Quarters, Camp, Valley Forge, May 5th, 1778.

It having pleased the Almighty Ruler of the Universe propitiously to defend the cause of the United American States, and finally, by raising us up a powerful friend among the princes of the earth, to establish our liberty and independence on a lasting foundation; it becomes us to set apart a day for gratefully acknowledging the Divine goodness, and celebrating the important event which we owe to His benign interposition."

At a signal from a single gun, Washington ordered:

The whole army will huzza—*Long live the King of France!* The artillery will then begin again, and fire thirteen rounds. This will be succeeded by a second general discharge of the musketry in a running fire—*Huzza! Long live the Friendly European Powers!* Then the last discharge of thirteen pieces of artillery will be given, followed by a general running fire—*Huzza for the American States!*

Four years later still, the Continental Congress in Philadelphia was able to proclaim another Thanksgiving in the name of a nation united and on its way to independence:

> It being the indispensable duty of all Nations, not only to offer up their supplications to ALMIGHTY GOD, the giver of all good, for his gracious assistance in a time of distress, but also in a solemn and public manner to give him praise for his goodness in general, and especially for great and signal interpositions of his providence in their behalf. . . .

Before the end of the Revolutionary War, in other words, one hundred and sixty-two years after the Pilgrim vanguard of Englishmen splashed ashore in Providence Bay, Americans, would-be citizens of a new nation less than two years from victory over the English monarch and his armies, had adapted the thanksgiving ritual to the high politics of nation building.

CHAPTER TEN

A Republic Gives Thanks

T HE NEXT HUNDRED YEARS SAW THE REVOLUTION, THE birth of the American Republic, and the sanctification of many of its patriotic myths and icons. The first call for observance after the Revolution came when President Washington, at the request of Congress, recommended Thursday, November 26, 1789, to the people of the United States "as a day of public thanksgiving and prayer to be observed by acknowledging with grateful hearts the many and signal favours of Almighty God."

The early years of the Republic saw a contest between two alternative modes of celebrating the first settlements. In 1769 Plymouth's Old Colony Club, made up of the tiny patriciate of *Mayflower* descendants, celebrated not the 1621 "First Thanksgiving" but the landing of 1620. At Thomas Southworth Howland's inn on December 22, 1769 (the anniversary of the landing in Plymouth), the members, who belonged to the elite of the little town, sat down to a dinner that included a "large baked Indian whortleberry pudding," dishes of "sauqetach" (squash), clams, oysters, and cod fish, a haunch of venison, plates of what were baldly described as "sea fowl," and "frost fish" and eels, an apple pie, cranberry tarts, and cheese.[1] No turkey!

This Old Colony dinner represented one tradition. Commemorating the landing of December 1620, it was masculine, elitist, eventually public, and unashamedly political. It was often called Forefathers' Day, but sometimes Embarkation Day or Landing Day. That was the spirit, for example, of the bicentennial celebration, not in 1821 but on December 22, 1820, in Plymouth. A newly inaugurated Pilgrim Society invited Daniel Webster to speak, which he did from a high oak pulpit in front of First Parish Church. Webster used the occasion to attack slavery. He and his audience knew, though he did not mention the fact explicitly, that surreptitious slave trading was happening no further than Brunswick, Rhode Island, once actually part of the territory of Plymouth colony. "It is not fit," Webster thundered, "that the land of the Pilgrims should bear the shame longer."

Again, in 1853, on August 1, Embarkation Day was celebrated with mammoth procession speeches and music. Why that particular day was chosen is not clear. It was neither the day the Pilgrims left Delfshaven (about July 22) nor the day they embarked from Southampton, which was about August 5. But in 1870 the two-hundred-and-fiftieth anniversary was celebrated in Plymouth on December 21. But the tercentenary was commemorated in 1921, not in 1920, marking the anniversary, not of the Pilgrims' landing, but of the (supposed) First Thanksgiving on an unknown date in 1621.

If Thanksgiving changed from being a public celebration, marked by the thunderous, Latinate oratory of Webster and his like, with fireworks and bunting and brass bands blaring out patriotic music, to something more domestic and more feminine, this was partly because of a new female influence, amounting in many cases to feminism, that was felt in New England in the generation before the Civil War. This was perhaps a product of New England's growing prosperity: Certainly it was connected with the moralism of Protestants and agnostic or theistic Transcendentalists. Thanksgiving was promoted, and transformed, by a number of high-minded, talented, and determined New England women. Margaret Fuller, the Transcendentalist friend of Ralph Waldo Emerson and Henry David Thoreau, journalist, feminist, and revolutionary in the cause of Italian liberty, wanted Thanksgiving to be more than just "a meeting of family and friends" for "a good dinner": She insisted that it must be an instrument of Reform.

Harriet Beecher Stowe, in her novel *Old Town Folks*, written in 1869, long after *Uncle Tom's Cabin*, evoked the spirit of a nineteenth-century New England Thanksgiving, the same atmosphere caught by a famous Currier & Ives print, *Home to Thanksgiving*, issued two years before Stowe's novel. In the print, now one of the most popular of all the partnership's hundreds of images, the grown-up son has arrived back, perhaps from the city, at the snow-covered family homestead. Between the house and the barn high mountains are visible, and the clouds are heavy with more snow to fall. An ox is dragging a heavy load of logs for the fire in the foreground. The horse and sleigh wait as the old folks pour out of the door onto the porch to greet the returned prodigal.

In *Old Town Folks*, a nostalgic recollection of the New England of her youth, Harriet Beecher Stowe, who had lived in Ohio for twenty years, made explicit the contrast between the military masculinity of other national holidays, and especially the Fourth of July, on the one hand, and on the other the domestic charm of Thanksgiving. She wrote:

There were some few national fêtes:—Election day, when the Governor took his seat with pomp and rejoicing, and all the housewives outdid themselves in election cake, and one or two training days, when all the children were refreshed, and our military ardor quickened, by the roll of drums, and the flash of steel bayonets, and marchings and evolutions—sometimes ending in that sublimest of military operations, a sham fight, in which nobody was killed. The Fourth of July took high rank, after the Declaration of Independence; but the king and high priest of all festivals was the autumn Thanksgiving.

When the apples were all gathered and the cider was all made, and the yellow pumpkins were rolled in from many a hill in billows of gold, and the corn was husked, and the labors of the season were done, and the warm, late days of Indian Summer came in, dreamy and calm and still, with just frost enough to crisp the ground of a morning, but with warm trances of benignant, sunny hours at noon, there came over the community a sort of genial repose of spirit,—a sense of something accomplished, and of a new golden mark made in advance on the calendar of life,—and the deacon began to say to the minister, of a Sunday, "I suppose it's about time for the Thanksgiving proclamation."

Then Stowe waxed lyrical about the preparations, the pies—chicken pies, apple pies, cherry and pumpkin pies—that emerged from the cool north room in the farmhouse.

But who shall do justice to the dinner, and describe the turkey, and chickens, and chicken pies, with all that endless variety of vegetables which the American soil and climate have contributed to the table, and which, without regard to the French doctrine of courses, were all piled together in jovial abundance upon the smoking board? There was much carving and laughing and talking and eating, and all showed that cheerful ability to despatch the provisions which was the ruling spirit of the hour. After the meat came the plum-puddings, and then the endless array of pies, till human nature was actually bewildered and overpowered by the tempting variety; and even we children turned from the profusion.

Lydia Maria Child, like Margaret Fuller and Harriet Beecher Stowe, was a woman of high culture, diverse achievement, and steadfast moral purpose. She was a feminist, an abolitionist, and a campaigner against the death penalty. Perhaps her most enduring achievement, though, was the poem everyone remembers called "A New England Boy's Thanksgiving."

> Over the river, and through the wood,
> To Grandfather's house we go!
> The horse knows the way,
> To carry the sleigh,
> Through the white and drifted snow.
> Over the river, and through the wood,
> To Grandfather's house away!
> We would not stop for doll or top,
> For this is Thanksgiving Day.

It might have been grandfather's house, it has been pointed out,[2] but it was very much grandmother's day.

> Over the river, and through the wood,
> When Grandmother sees us come,
> She will say, "Oh, dear,
> The children are here,
> bring a pie for every one."
> Over the river, and through the wood,
> Now Grandmother's cap I spy!
> Hurrah for the fun!
> Is the pudding done?
> Hurrah for the pumpkin pie!

The decisive advocacy for a national thanksgiving holiday was another New England woman, also a journalist. This was Sarah Josepha Hale, otherwise best known as the author of the unforgettable verses that begin, "Mary had a little lamb."

She was born Sarah Buell on a New Hampshire farm in 1788.[3] Her father, who had fought in the Revolutionary War, opened a tavern that did not prosper. Sarah married a lawyer and freemason, David Hale, and together they started a literary club and she experimented with writing verse. In 1822, Hale died of pneumonia and she found herself a widow, aged thirty-four, with five children. Her husband's Masonic brethren set her and her sister-in-law up in a millinery business, and she published some poems and a novel about slavery, *Northwood*. An Episcopal minister, Reverend John L. Blake, was sufficiently impressed by her writing to offer her the editorship of a new magazine he was starting, aimed at women readers. The first woman editor of a magazine in the United States, she left her children to be brought up by relatives and moved to Boston. The magazine was called the *Ladies Magazine and Literary Gazette*, later called the *American Ladies Magazine*.

Although she was not a supporter of women's suffrage, Hale worked tirelessly for women's education. She worked with Matthew Vassar, the founder of Vassar College, where she insisted that preference should be given to qualified women instructors where they could be found; and she helped Elizabeth Blackwell to become the first American woman doctor. She was also involved in a number of civic and patriotic causes. She founded the Seaman's Society, and helped to raise money to preserve both the Bunker Hill monument and Mount Vernon.

In the late 1830s, financial difficulties led to the absorption of her magazine by Louis Godey's *Lady's Book*, which she edited until the magazine was bought by Frank Munsey in 1877. She died in 1879 at the age of ninety-one. She was not only one of the longest serving, but also one of the most influential, editors in nineteenth-century America. *Lady's Book* became the "bible of the Victorian parlor." It reached a circulation of 150,000 and exerted a steady influence on behalf of the education and improvement of women in many ways. Where, before she became editor in 1836, *Lady's Book* devoted most of its space to recipes and fashions in hats and gowns, Hale brought in the best writers of the day, including Washington Irving, William Cullen Bryan, Edgar Allan Poe, Longfellow, and Emerson. The subject matter became appropriately more serious, and one of the magazine's constant campaigns was on behalf of the New England custom of observing Thanksgiving.

As early as 1827, when she wrote *Northwood*, and before she became an editor, Hale preached the virtues of the Thanksgiving holiday. "We have too few holidays," she wrote in *Northwood*. "Thanksgiving like the Fourth of July should be considered a national festival and observed by all our people." She saw the festival as a spiritual weapon to combat the divisions that were leading the nation towards civil war. "There is a deep moral influence," she wrote, "in these periodical seasons of rejoicing, in which whole communities participate. They bring out . . . the best sympathies in our natures." In an editorial written before the war, she called on "the people of all the States and Territories [to] sit down together to the 'feast of fat things' and drink in the sweet draught of joy and gratitude to the Divine giver of all our blessings, the pledge of renewed love to the Union." Those sentiments, it seemed to her, were even more relevant once the irrepressible conflict had broken into war. Over a quarter of a century she wrote to dozens of senators, congressmen, and other public men to advocate making the Thanksgiving holiday an official national celebration. She lobbied five presidents in this cause. But it was not until the supreme crisis of the Civil War that she wrote another letter that succeeded in persuading Abraham Lincoln to take her advice.

Lincoln's proclamations and other political pronouncements in the course of the war were, of course, conditioned by the fortunes of the struggle. Thus, when, in September 1862, Lincoln read to his cabinet a preliminary draft of an emancipation proclamation, Secretary of State William Seward suggested it should not be issued until after a great victory, and it was the battle of Antietam that gave him his opportunity. The formal proclamation was not issued until New Year's Day 1863. The twin victories of Vicksburg and Gettysburg, in July 1863, opened the way to victory, but before Lincoln could give his Gettysburg Address, on November 19, things took a turn for the worse. The army of the Tennessee was mauled at Chicakamauga on September 19 and 20, in one of the bloodiest battles of the entire war. After Gettysburg, General George Meade failed to press home the Union's advantage in Virginia. It has even been suggested that the proclamation of an official, national celebration of thanksgiving was the beginning of Lincoln's campaign for the presidential election of 1864. Issued almost three months after the battle of Gettysburg, and just over six weeks before Lincoln's unforgettable speech at the dedication of the Gettysburg cemetery, it was more probably motivated by the need to maintain the civilian morale of a Union whose ultimate victory might now be inevitable, but where the costs and travails of the war were bitterly discouraging. Lincoln was always acutely aware of the connection between civilian morale and military victory in a great citizen army, and he was particularly sensitive to the moral sensibilities of the New England Christian intelligentsia and to that New England Protestant tradition to which, after all, the nation owed Thanksgiving in the first place. The decision to make Thanksgiving a national holiday illustrates the two sides of Lincoln's genius: the moral prophet and the shrewd politician.

"In the midst of a civil war of unequaled magnitude and severity," he wrote, ". . . needful diversions of wealth and strength from the field of peaceful industry to the national defense have not arrested the plow, the shuttle, or the ship; the ax had enlarged the borders of our settlements, . . . the country, rejoicing in the consciousness of augmented strength and vigor, is permitted to expect continuance of years with large increase of freedom." These, Lincoln reminded his countrymen, were "the gracious gifts of the Most High God. . . . They should be solemnly, reverently and gratefully acknowledged." So he invited his fellow citizens to observe the last Thursday of November as a day of thanksgiving and praise "to our beneficent Father who dwelleth in the heavens."

A year later, President Lincoln repeated his Thanksgiving proclamation, and this time it was celebrated in a way that reflected the welling up of patriotic sentiment that would reach its climax a year later in the great victory marches of the Grand Army of the Republic. A well-known New York editor, George Washington Blunt, came up with an original proposal. Something should be done, he said, for the "Army and Navy" for Thanksgiving, "not only to aid them in keeping the day properly, but to show them they are remembered at home." He proposed to send the troops "poultry and pies, or puddings, all cooked, ready for use." He estimated it would take 50,000 turkeys and a like number of pies to feed the 220,000 men of the Army and Navy besieging Richmond. "This seems to be a big undertaking," he wrote, "but I do not see any difficulty in carrying it out." The food could be prepared and boxed up by those who could afford it, and shipped from New York a few days in advance, in time to be distributed the day before. If the idea has merit, he wrote, "I am ready to do my best with others to put it through."

The Union League Club of New York City, whose members could well afford it, launched a public campaign to provide Thanksgiving dinner for Union soldiers and sailors. Theodore Roosevelt's father was the treasurer of this effort. "We desire," the club resolved, "that on the twenty-fourth day of November there shall be no soldier in the Army of the Potomac, the James, the Shenandoah, and no sailor in the North Atlantic Squadron who does not receive tangible evidence that those for whom he is periling his life, remember him. . . . We ask primarily for donations of cooked poultry and other proper meats, as well as for mince pies, sausages and fruits. . . . To those who are unable to send donations in kind, we appeal for generous contributions in money."

In three weeks, the club collected over $57,000 to buy 150,000 pounds of turkey, and another 225,000 pounds of poultry was donated in kind, not to mention cakes, gingerbread, pickles, apples, vegetables, cheese, and mince pies. New York's contributions were cooked, wrapped in white paper, packed in straw in boxes or barrels, and marked "Our Defenders, City Point." Transportation companies volunteered to ship the materials by rail and steamship. New York was not alone. Ladies of Jersey City raised $1,500 to buy cigars for the troops, while the citizens of Orange, New Jersey, sent bags of tomatoes. An army apple fund was created, and Ohioans decided to help the wives and families of men at the front with much-needed money.

Captain George F. Noyes reported from General Phil Sheridan's Army of the Shenandoah that "the want of proper appliances compelled most of the men to broil or stew their turkeys, but everyone seemed fully satisfied, and appreciated the significance of this sympatric thank-offering from the loyal North. One soldier said to me, 'It isn't the turkey, but the idea that we care for.'"

Thanksgiving was essentially a New England custom. It was spread to the Middle West by New England migrants, and from there reached the South. By the 1850s, according to Matthew Dennis, Virginia, Mississippi, Louisiana, Texas, Arkansas, and Missouri had all officially celebrated Thanksgiving at least once. Yet as a Yankee festival it was suspect, when not actually offensive, to many Southerners. In 1853, for example, a governor of Virginia, Joseph Johnson, refused to declare a thanksgiving on the grounds that it would breach the Constitution ban on an establishment of religion. The real reason for southern hostility was more that

Thanksgiving had become identified with New Englanders' abolitionist rhetoric. Another antebellum governor of Virginia, Henry Wise, rejected the festival as "theatrical national claptrap" that was notoriously used to advance "other causes," meaning antislavery.

Still the Confederacy, as well as the Union, celebrated its triumphs with thanksgiving ceremonies. The confederate victory at Bull Run in 1861 was marked in this way. Jefferson Davis also declared a Thanksgiving day, for November 16, 1864, a day "specially devoted to the worship of Almighty God," that the people of the Confederacy would join together in prayer that God would, inter alia, "restore peace to our beloved country, healing its bleeding wounds and securing to us the continued enjoyment of our right of self-government and independence."

By the Gilded Age, Thanksgiving was firmly established as a national festival, authorized by presidential proclamation, and welcomed North and South as a peculiarly warm and intimate event. In the late nineteenth century, it began to acquire a new and special significance as a festival of national inclusiveness. Up to the Civil War, the great majority of immigrants who came to the United States came from the British Isles, especially from Ireland, and from Northern Europe. Although the Irish were Catholics, they were for the most part English-speaking and they were familiar (too familiar, many would have said) with Anglo-Saxon folkways. For twenty years after the war, most immigrants continued to come from northern Europe, especially from Germany and Scandinavia, and most of them shared the Protestant religion of the American majority.

From the 1880s on, however, more and more immigrants came from southern and eastern Europe. They were Italian, Polish, Hungarian or Croatian Catholics, Russian or Serbian Orthodox, and Jews from everywhere in central and eastern Europe. At first, Thanksgiving seemed to some of them an unfamiliar Protestant festival. But gradually they came to feel a special affection for the friendly and inclusive spirit of the holiday, which celebrates family feeling without making the specifically Christian and Protestant demands of Christmas.

Strict Jews, with their own rich tradition of holidays and thanksgiving, have sometimes worried about whether it was appropriate to celebrate Thanksgiving, and have mostly decided that it is. As early as 1868, only five years after Lincoln's proclamation, Governor John Geary of Pennsylvania, proclaimed that his state would observe a Thanksgiving holiday on November 26th. He recommended "that the people of this Commonwealth refrain from their usual avocations and pursuits, and assemble at their chosen place of worship," to "praise the name of God and magnify Him with thanksgiving." And he called on Pennsylvanians to pray that "our paths through life may be directed by the example and instructions of the Redeemer." Seven of Philadelphia's rabbis, including Sabato Morais, later the first head of the Jewish theological Seminary of America, and Marcus Jastrow, father of the great orientalist Morris Jastrow, protested Geary's proclamation as "an encroachment upon the immunities we are entitled to share" with all Pennsylvanians. Moreover they pointed out that "the freedom-loving authors of the American Constitution" opened to all "the avenues of greatness." The day might come when the governor of the state might be a Jew or even a "free-thinker."

To this day, some religious Jews continue to worry about Thanksgiving as a secular or even a Christian festival. Michael Broyde, a law professor at Emory University, and a *dayan*, or judge, in the Beth Din, the religious court of America, reassures them. After going through the arguments of a number of learned rabbis, he concludes that "Halakhah permits one to have a private Thanksgiving celebration with one's Jewish or secular friends and family" and he adds that "for reasons related to citizenship and the gratitude we feel towards the United States government, I would even suggest that such conduct is wise and proper."

Many, perhaps most, American Jews follow Professor Broyde's advice. Steven Greenberg, for example, of the National Jewish Center for Learning and Leadership, has written that "Thanksgiving always had the feel of a liberated *Pesach*," and points out that the same family members would "show up for my mother's cooking on both holidays." In his family, parents, grandparents, and other relatives would tell a story of coming to America, a story of trials and difficulties and of thanks and gratitude to this country for its freedoms and opportunities. "Our family Thanksgiving *seder* rarely has taken longer than fifteen minutes," he said. "But it is enough to make us all aware of the story, our Pilgrims' story, our American story, and our Jewish-American story." For such reasons, given their previous experience of persecution and Holocaust, Jews may appreciate Thanksgiving even more than most gentile families.

BY THE LATE NINETEENTH CENTURY, THE THANKSGIVING holiday was already beginning to be associated with entertainment in general and in particular sport. For ten or fifteen years, colleges had been challenging one another to one version or another of the two English football codes, Association (or "soccer"), a kicking-only game, and rugby, where a player could carry the ball and run with it. Constant disagreements about the rules, the number of players allowed on each side and the scoring systems made for endless argument. In 1876, the centennial year, four Ivy League universities formed the Intercollegiate Football Association. The final was held on Thanksgiving. In the 1880s, largely under the influence of Yale's Walter Camp, the distinctively American game of football emerged, with eleven on a side and forward passing allowed. By the 1890s, according to one historian, as many as forty thousand spectators turned up to watch the game and bet heavily on its result. (In those days, football was still a college, not a professional sport, and the top teams were the Princeton Tigers and the Yale Bulldogs.) In 1893 the New York *Herald* went so far as to say that "Thanksgiving is no longer a solemn festival to God for mercies given. . . . It is a holiday granted by the State and the Nation to see a game of football." When professional football did come along, in 1934, its sponsor scheduled a game between the Detroit Lions and the Chicago Bears for Thanksgiving Day. It was broadcast coast to coast. Today NFL football on Thanksgiving is a national tradition almost as sacred as turkey and cranberry sauce or pumpkin pie.

The last official change in the observation of Thanksgiving came in 1939. The reason was simple, if in many people's opinion a tad undignified. In 1933 and again in 1939, Thanksgiving fell on November 30. Already in 1933, retailers had noticed that, in a nation mired in deep recession, where people didn't start their Christmas shopping until after Thanksgiving, retail sales were painfully down. (Since 1924 the annual Macy's Parade in New York City on Thanksgiving Day was considered the opening of the Christmas shopping season, even though Thanksgiving itself, compared to other holidays, remained and has remained relatively free from commercialization.) In August 1939, Lew Hahn, general manager of the Retail Dry Goods Association, sent a message to Secretary of Commerce Harry Hopkins that although he didn't dare bring this to the president's attention, a late Thanksgiving might have a "possible adverse effect on the production and distribution of holiday goods." Roosevelt, alerted by Hopkins, his closest associate, responded. He announced that henceforth Thanksgiving would be, not on the last Thursday, but on the fourth. The move was popular with retailers, but not with everyone else. Indeed a poll showed that 62 percent of Americans disapproved. Some had to reschedule holiday travel plans. The mayor of Atlantic City was so annoyed that he called the new holiday "Franksgiving," and there were States that simply ignored the change of date. Governor W. Lee "Pass the Biscuits Pappy" O'Daniel of Texas[4] decreed two Thanksgivings, one for Roosevelt, as was said, and one for the traditional Texas–Texas A & M football game. By 1942, Roosevelt acknowledged his mistake. But when Congress changed the law in 1941, the holiday continued to be scheduled for the fourth Thursday in November.

Epilogue:
The Invention of
a Tradition

IN THE 1980S A GROUP OF BRITISH HISTORIANS PUBLISHED
an influential book called *The Invention of Tradition*. They
pointed out, often with wit as well as scholarship, that many nations cherish as part of their national myth events that didn't hap-
pen, or things whose nature was far different from what has been
remembered. Some of their examples were comparatively trivial
and even funny. Hugh Trevor-Roper, for example, revealed that
the Scots' beloved kilt did not date back to the mists of the Celtic
twilight; it was invented by an English industrialist because it was
less likely than the traditional plaid wrap to get in his workers' way
when they were working in his sawmill. David Cannadine showed
how for the first three-quarters of the nineteenth century British
coronations and similar royal occasions were notoriously chaotic
and Englishmen of the day prided themselves on their lack of interest in such flummeries. They should be left to what a British
nobleman dismissed with an audible sniff as "people of a southern
climate and of non-Teutonic parentage." The monarchy, in Queen
Victoria's age, was far less popular than it became after World War

II. Its home, Windsor, a standby for modern tourists, was so obscure in those days that it could be dismissed by *Punch* magazine as "an obscure Berkshire village noted only for an old castle with no sanitary arrangements."

It is easy to think of other examples of invented tradition. It is said, no doubt apocryphally, that there are colleges where signs advise the visitor that "There is a tradition that visitors do not walk on the grass. This tradition will take effect from tomorrow." The famous Lloyd's of London insurance market loves to talk of its origins in the merchants' coffeehouses of eighteenth-century London, but most of its working parts date back no farther than the 1880s. The French historian Pierre Nora, editor of a voluminous series called *Les Lieux de Mémoire*—which translates as "places of memory," but means something closer to "heritage sites"—has explored, with a team of researchers, the changing fortunes of such classic icons of French nationalism as the *tricouleur* flag and the Marseillaise, demonstrating how often raucous revolutionary anger has been converted into safely bourgeois national unity. Bastille Day, France's cherished national holiday on July 14, was introduced not in 1789, when the almost empty Bastille was liberated, but in 1880.

In passing, the learned editor of the *Invention of Tradition* volume, the distinguished historian Eric Hobsbawm, mentioned Thanksgiving. The invented traditions of the U.S.A. in the late nineteenth century, he suggested, were "primarily designed" to deal with what he called the basic problem, once secession had been defeated, namely "how to assimilate . . . an almost unmanageable influx" of immigrants. "The immigrants were encouraged to accept rituals commemorating the history of the nation—the Revolution and its founding fathers (the Fourth of July) and the Protestant Anglo-Saxon tradition (Thanksgiving Day)—as indeed they did, since these now became holidays and occasions for public and private festivity."[1]

Thanksgiving was not a wholly "invented" tradition. Still less was it "primarily designed" to Americanize immigrants. It was designed neither by an individual nor by a committee. In the late-nineteenth and the twentieth centuries it was embraced by immigrants with love, not foisted on them by manipulative masters. It was rather a very ancient tradition adapted to fit the emotional, religious, and national needs of the American people in each generation as they increased, multiplied, and spread westward, and in so doing created a new civilization, at once recognizably European in origin and yet unmistakably new in character.

Even so, it is hard to deny that in the popular Thanksgiving as it is celebrated, but also as it is promoted and described, in newspapers and schools, in commercial advertising and political discourse, there are invented elements.

It would be a brave historian who would accept Winslow's feasting as the direct ancestor of the modern Thanksgiving, just as it is time to discard the picture of Pilgrims marching to land by way of the plump little boulder of Plymouth Rock from a *Mayflower* anchored hundreds of yards offshore in Plymouth Bay. The First Thanksgiving must join Plymouth Rock and Parson Weems's story of the young George Washington and his father's cherry tree among the pious fictions of the American political religion. They are not historically provable events, but powerful images useful for inspiring nationalist loyalties: like the story of the English King Alfred burning the cakes; or Robert Bruce and the spider who said that if he would be king of Scotland he must "Try and try and try again"; or the legend that in Germany's hour of need Frederick Barbarossa will arise from his cavern under the Kyffhaüser mountain and save the German *Volk*.

The Winslow First Thanksgiving, in short, is a fiction. But that does not mean that it is in any way fraudulent or deceptive. On the contrary, the myth of Thanksgiving is a powerful and virtuous symbol. It expresses some of the simplest, the most decent, and the noblest feelings. It is a far more attractive thing to say thanks for prosperity and freedom from tyranny than to triumph over defeated enemies—to call on the Creator (as does the embarrassing second verse of the British national anthem) to "frustrate their knavish tricks," or indeed to pray, as does the *Marseillaise*, that "an impure blood not sully our furrows." One can deconstruct the idea of Thanksgiving as much as one likes. It remains, not a hymn to battle or violence, not a festival of national pride and superiority, but a domestic celebration of gratitude, humility, and inclusiveness. These are not qualities for which anyone need apologize.

Now Thanksgiving, the avatar of the harvest home, celebrates the gathering not of scattered crops but of disparate people. It is the holiday when family comes home. That's why Halliburton's gesture in 2005, however well intentioned, slightly missed the point. When they sought to dramatize their connection to the war in Iraq by boasting of their success in bringing Thanksgiving to young service men and women, they overlooked the fact that it was not the turkey that the troops were missing as much as home and family.

Halliburton served "300,000 pounds of turkey, 150,000 pounds of boneless ham," not presumably to Muslim friends and neighbors, and much else besides. Somehow that seemed a little different from Theodore Roosevelt Sr., father of the president, and his friends at the Union League club sending turkeys to the boys in blue shivering in the trenches in front of Richmond.

In their many bases and assignments around the world, CNN reported, U.S. soldiers, sailors, airmen, and marines did their best to come as close as possible to the holiday they would have had at home, and at the same time shared it if they could with local people. In Kosovo a National Guard lieutenant-colonel from Kansas who is a teacher back home served turkey, cranberry sauce, and cinnamon rolls on blue plastic plates to seventeen ethnic Serb students at their school desks in the snow-covered village of Vrbo-vac and tried to apply the message of the Thanksgiving story to the ethnic quarrels of Kosovo. In Afghanistan senior officers served turkey and pumpkin pie to enlisted men, some of them with their weapons slung over their shoulders, at the Bagram base, while at a base in Kyrgyztan troops decorated their tanks as a turkey, a house, and a satellite dish in a brave imitation of Macy's traditional floats in the New York Thanksgiving Day parade.

"We feel like we're protecting our friends, families and loved ones back home," said a military chaplain in Iraq. "On the other hand, the holidays can be a somber, sad day for soldiers away from home," many of whom were away from home for the first time. "I miss not seeing my little daughter around the Thanksgiving table," said a twenty-two-year-old corporal from Columbus, Ohio, in Iraq; his daughter is two. "I could be sitting on the couch at home watching football with my dad," said an even younger Marine from Petaluma, California, who was spending his first-ever Christmas away from home on the bleak and dangerous desert frontier between Iraq and Syria.

These Americans far from home, because of a war not everyone back home supported, took their Thanksgiving seriously. As did many new Americans, who found it easy to relate their own experience to the story they had been told of Pilgrims venturing to an unknown and perilous land in search of freedom and finding a modest prosperity there.

In San José, California, better known to the world as Silicon Valley, the local paper found three orphans from the brutal civil war in Liberia—Mariama, Sidikie, and Ansumama Dolleh—shopping for Thanksgiving with their foster mother, Tracy Weiss, a divorced mother of two sons from Los Altos. Mariama, aged 18, and her seventeen-year-old brother Sidikie heaved an enormous plastic-coated turkey into a shopping trolley. "I've heard about this turkey," said their younger brother warily. "When I've experienced it, I'll have a better idea of what it's about." "This is my favorite American holiday," said Weiss. "It's all about good stuff and nothing about what's wrong with the world."

At the other side of the country, other new Americans were discovering the pleasures, and the philosophical meanings, of Thanksgiving. Once again, as in the late-nineteenth century, more than one-third of New York City's population is foreign born. A *New York Times* reporter, called Manny Fernandez, found eleven-year-old Julie Sorokurs in Sheepshead Bay, Brooklyn, helping to make apple pie and pinning together black paper to make Pilgrim hats. Her father, Vladimir, came to America from Russia in 1998. "She has to adopt everything," he says of his daughter. "She's American." Mr. Fernandez found similar responses in families from Colombia, from Uzbekistan, and from Palestine. It was, he reported, a "cross-cultural hodgepodge holiday." Like Jessie Mangaliman, the reporter in San José, Fernandez found culinary variations. A Mexican family ate turkey with *mole* (a hot sauce), and Afghans preferred rice to potatoes; a Palestinian mother said she would eat anything, even turkey, so long as the meat was *halal*, correctly butchered according to Muslim law. In the early twenty-first century, just as a hundred years earlier, now in California as well as in New York, immigrant children who had learned about Thanksgiving at school were teaching this American tradition to their parents. A fourteen-year-old from Ukraine remembered her first Thanksgiving in 1999. The family watched the Macy's parade on television and put turkey decorations in the windows. She found it exciting. "The Pilgrims were becoming Americans, and now, so were we."

The Pilgrims didn't eat turkey, and it took their descendants five generations to become Americans. But that does not matter, least of all to the new Americans for whom the holiday is a warm and potent symbol of acceptance, of goodwill, of hope.

For Thanksgiving 1869, *Harper's Weekly* produced as its centerfold a drawing by Thomas Nast called *Uncle Sam's Thanksgiving Dinner*. It is an image, not of a typical American family of the day sitting down to dinner, but of the family of man. Twenty-six figures—men, women, and children—are drawn. A recognizably American man carves the turkey, but the guests represent Nast's idea of ethnic diversity. A young white woman sits conversing pleasantly with an African man on her left and a Chinese man with a long pigtail reaching over his shoulder and down the back of his chair. A dark, bearded man sits between the Chinese wife and a woman with her hair covered with a head cloth, perhaps from the Balkans. To their right sits a lady of Spain with mantilla and fan, opposite a Native American with a single feather sticking up from his head, and stereotypical figures of many other nationalities—an obese Turk, a bearded Russian, perhaps, and a Victorian Englishman's caricature of an Irish boy—share the feast. Nast was not in the habit of leaving any doubt about the message he meant to convey. The table center is labeled "Universal Suffrage," and in the bottom left-hand corner of the drawing Nast has written the words "Come One, Come All," balanced in the bottom right-hand corner with the word "Free and Equal." Portraits of Washington, flanked by Lincoln and Ulysses S. Grant, hang from the wall behind the diners, and behind the carver there is a painting of New York harbor. Below the shipping are the words, "Castle Garden," the place through which immigrants entered the country before Ellis Island took its place in 1890; and on the frame above the picture is the single word "Welcome." Thanksgiving, for Nast, has become a symbol of the promise of American life to all the world.

Nast was a Radical Republican, a nineteenth-century liberal whose father, a trombonist in a military band, left Germany in

THOMAS NAST
(Illustration provided courtesy of HarpWeek, LLC)

1849, after the collapse of the 1848 revolution, and who traveled to Sicily to report sympathetically on Garibaldi's invasion of Italy. The formative experience of his life was his work as a war artist covering the Civil War, and it was his 1864 cartoon fiercely denouncing *Compromise with the South*, endlessly reprinted by the Republicans in Lincoln's re-election campaign, that brought him national fame. Nast was certainly an American patriot, with an immigrant's fierce love of his adopted country. But no one could accuse him of turning a blind eye to the failings of his beloved land. After the war he turned his caustic pencil to the depredations of William Marcy "Boss" Tweed. It is said that Tweed told his Tammany braves to "Stop them damned pictures. I don't care so much what the papers say about me. My constituents can't read. But, damn it, they can see pictures!" Nast's pictures haunted him:

The story goes that when Tweed escaped from jail and fled to Spain, he was arrested by a Spanish customs officer who couldn't read English but recognized Tweed from Nast's pictures in *Harper's*.

Nast's vision of a cosmic Thanksgiving, at which all the nations of the earth are bid to sit down in peace to share in the plenty of America, still has immense power today. Wherever there are still poor and huddled masses, in South America, in Africa, in Asia, there are those who dream of sitting down to eat Thanksgiving as Americans. It has to be said, though, that the meaning of Thanksgiving has been drastically changed between the vision of Pastor John Robinson and that of Thomas Nast. Robinson, Brewster, Bradford, and their companions had many motives for sailing to Plymouth, including fear of persecution by Arminian churchmen in England or the Spanish Inquisition in Holland, hopes of plenty, and the dream of building a church in the wilderness as God had desired them to do. Never in their generation or for generations to come was there any idea that they were to lay the foundations for a universal refuge. They gave thanks for their own salvation and for the good fortune their God had vouchsafed them—when they were not fasting and humbling themselves to ward off the heavy hand of a jealous God and to deserve his loving kindness.

Between William Bradford and Thomas Nast there fell great historic transformations. There was the Enlightenment, for one thing, the "Lights" (as the French called them) that lifted from European minds that obsessive fear of divine wrath that oppressed them in the century and a half after the Reformation, an age of brilliant creativity and expansion, but also of religious war and persecution. Then, too, came the twin revolutions, first the American Revolution with its vision of people governed only with their own consent, then the French with an ideal—imperfectly realized, like all ideals—of freedom and equality, and a fraternity that stretched wider than a single people. Third, between the Pilgrims and the liberals of nineteenth-century America there lay the great fact of America itself, a continent largely and, it must be said, ruthlessly cleared of its native occupants, so that it now stretched from ocean to ocean as an apparently inexhaustible garden to be tilled and used by land-hungry Europeans. And in 1869 Thomas Nast had the imagination to look even further forward into a future when not only Europeans, but others from even hungrier continents would want to give thanks for sharing in the abundance of America.

The meaning of Thanksgiving, after all, has not been invented, even if the First Thanksgiving was nothing of the kind and few ancient turkey bones can be found, however hard you dig, along Plymouth's Town Brook. It has been adapted to the changing beliefs and aspirations of a society that has itself been utterly transformed, not once but a dozen times over, in almost four hundred years. The new urban, industrial America that was coming into existence in Thomas Nast's lifetime has gone, its smoking chimneys replaced by oil, then by natural gas, its railroads and electric telegraph replaced by automobiles and airplanes and digital messages, infinitely fast. Its relationship with the rest of the world has been turned inside out. Where America was first a wilderness where Pilgrims sought refuge, then an almost demilitarized sanctuary from the world's great powers, now it has become the greatest of those powers. The whole texture of the modern Thanksgiving holiday at home—largely secular in spite of the nation's still cherished religious traditions, and subtly pervaded, from food to football, by the influence of corporate media—is unrecognizable, not just from the perspective of Thomas Nast or Winslow Homer, but from that of Norman Rockwell and his New England family, celebrating with genteel joviality their freedom from want, their gratitude for American freedom in a world threatened by dictatorship.

Yet if almost everything about Thanksgiving has changed, several times over, those New Americans, from the barrios of Latin America and the bleak housing projects of what was once the Soviet empire, may have grasped the central meaning of what longer established, more blasé Americans may sometimes forget. It is, after all, a breathtaking story. No generous heart can fail to watch with admiration as a tiny band of men and women, determined to follow what they believe to be the ordinances of their God, entrust themselves to the wild, freezing ocean; confront disease, starvation, ferocious enemies, and justified fear; and succeed in building their church and their settlement. There is a painful fascination in the tragic dénouement of their failed attempts to follow their conscience in their dealings with the Indians. They were not perfect, as they acknowledged themselves with their habit of prayer and self-humiliation. But who can fail to wish them well, or to join in their thanksgiving at the mere fact of their survival? And who cannot feel that the Thanksgiving that grew out of that is a saner basis for national pride than dynastic pomp or military self-congratulation?

It is good to celebrate the public glories and the promise of American life with fireworks and speeches, better still to commemorate the mysterious cycle of life, the parade of the generations, and the fragile miracle of plenty, in the small warm circle of family, the building brick of which all prouder towers have always been constructed.

Notes

PROLOGUE: THANKSGIVING

1. William Bradford, *Of Plymouth Plantation 1620–1647*, ed. Samuel Eliot Morison (New York: Random House, 1952), 63.

2. Dwight B. Heath (ed.), *Mourt's Relation: A Journal of the Pilgrims at Plymouth* (Bedford, MA: Applewood Books, 1963), 82.

3. Edward Winslow, *Good Newes from New England* (Bedford, MA: Applewood Books, [1624] 1996).

4. William DeLoss Love, *The Fast and Thanksgiving Days of New England* (Boston, New York: Houghton and Mifflin, 1895).

THE REFORMATION

1. See Walter Prescott Webb, *The Great Frontier* (Austin, TX: University of Texas Press, 1952).

2. Quoted in Philip Mansel, *Constantinople: City of the World's Desire, 1453–1924* (London: John Murray, 1995), 4.

3. Diarmaid MacCulloch, *The Reformation* (New York: Viking, 2003), 55.

4. Two good recent histories of exploration and the origins of the slave trade are Hugh Thomas, *The Slave Trade* (New York: Simon & Schuster, 1997), and Robin Blackburn, *The Making of New World Slavery: From the Baroque to the Modern, 1492–1800* (London: Verso, 1997).

5. Hugh Thomas (*Slave Trade*, 861–62) devotes a note in an appendix to estimates of the number of slaves transported. He concludes that although it

is not necessary to know the precise number "the approximate figure would seem to be something like eleven million slaves, give or take 500,000."

6. This account of the English Reformation and the Elizabethan Settlement is based on the following: Owen Chadwick, *The Reformation* (London: Penguin, 1990); Patrick Collinson, *The Elizabethan Puritan Movement* (London: Jonathan Cape, 1967); A. G. Dickens, *The English Reformation*, rev. ed. (London: Batsford, 1989); A. F. Scott Pearson, *Thomas Cartwright and Elizabethan Puritanism* (Cambridge: Cambridge University Press, 1925); MacCulloch, *Reformation.*

7. Dickens, *English Reformation*, 20–21.

8. The epidemiology of syphilis is contested. Some authorities believe it was found on both sides of the Atlantic. (It is not easy to distinguish it in archeological evidence from other diseases such as yaws and even leprosy.) Others believe it was brought to Europe, as was thought for a long time, only after Columbus' voyages. It is also possible that the disease was originally European, but Europeans had developed an immunity to it, so that only when it had devastated populations with no immunity in the Caribbean did it return to Europe with such terrible results.

9. At the peace of Augsburg in 1555 it was decided as between Lutherans and Catholics that *cuius regio, eius religio,* that is, "whose rule, his religion." In 1648, in the treaty of Westphalia that ended the Thirty Years War, the principle was extended to Calvinists.

10. MacCulloch, *Reformation*, 382.

11. Collinson, *Elizabethan Puritan Movement*, 27: "The Bible . . . this was the only authority which the puritan acknowledged in matters of religion."

12. The lengthy title on the title page began "Actes and Monuments of these latter and perilous dayes touching matters of the Church. . . ." But it was always called Foxe's *Book of Martyrs.*

13. Possibly in order to meet resentment of her position as a woman, she changed her title from "Head" of the Church, which her father had been, to "Supreme Governor."

14. That is, the Church of England claimed that its priests were ordained by others who could trace their own ordination back to Jesus's apostles, just as Catholic priests claimed to be able to do.

15. The historian Diarmaid MacCulloch, in particular, has argued that the Calvinist character of the sixteenth-century Church of England was concealed by nineteenth-century Anglo-Catholic historians who minimized the extent to which the English Reformation marked a decisive break with

Catholicism. See Diarmaid MacCulloch, "The Myth of the English Reformation," *History Today* 41, 7 (July 1991): 28–35.

16. Of a list of 28 candidates for bishoprics given her by Lord Leicester early in her reign, 21 had been in exile; of the 21 men she appointed to bishoprics, 13 had been with Calvin and his successor Beza in Zurich. Collinson, *Elizabethan Puritan Movement*, 49; Henry M. Dexter and Norton Dexter, *The England and Holland of the Pilgrims* (Boston: Houghton Mifflin, 1905), 93.

17. Collinson, *Elizabethan Puritan Movement*, 55.

18. Notably the Russell family, ancestors of the modern dukes of Bedford. They had great influence in the West Country, whose small market towns and seaports were overrepresented in Parliament, with the result that Francis Russell, earl of Bedford, who had bought vast monastic estates from Henry VIII when the monasteries were dissolved, controlled a significant proportion of all the members of Queen Elizabeth's first Parliament.

19. "Troublechurch" Browne, as he was known, started a Separatist congregation in 1581, was reported to the Privy Council by the bishop of Norwich, and left for Middleburg in Holland. The Dutch found him disruptive, and he moved to Scotland, where he was put in jail. In 1585, after four years on the wrong side of the law, he rejoined the Church of England, though two men were burned as heretics for distributing his writings.

20. Thomas Cartwright was born in Royston, near Cambridge, probably in 1535. He entered Cambridge University in 1550, and became a fellow of Trinity College. He later traveled to Geneva, served as chaplain to the archbishop of Armagh in Ireland, and impressed Queen Elizabeth on a visit to Cambridge. He was later Lady Margaret professor of divinity, but fell out with John Whitgift (master of Trinity, and later archbishop of Canterbury), and was deprived of his chair in 1570, and of his fellowship in 1571. He eventually returned to Geneva and was imprisoned as a Puritan from 1590 to 1592. He died in 1603.

21. "Anabaptist" or "rebaptizer" was a name given by their enemies to followers of many variations of radical Protestantism in Switzerland, Germany, and the Low Countries in the sixteenth century. They traced their origins to those in Zurich who rebelled against the authority of the Reformer Zwingli. They believed that salvation came *sola scriptura* and *sola fidei* ("only by scripture" and "only by faith") and they rejected infant baptism. They were persecuted with hideous cruelty, especially by Charles V and Philip II, and most of all after a mad Anabaptist, John of Leiden, set up

an authoritarian Anabaptist republic, utterly out of line with the pacifist Anabaptist tradition, in the German city of Munster.

22. Francis Dillon, *A Place for Habitation: The Pilgrim Fathers and Their Quest* (London: Hutchinson, 1973), 77, citing George Johnson, *A Discourse of Some Trouble*, a somewhat salacious account of the internal scandals and disputes of the "Ancient Church."

23. That is, January 14 then, by Old Style, the Julian calendar, before the introduction of the reformed, Gregorian, calendar, not adopted in England until 1752.

24. Dr. John Rainolds and Dr. Sparks, both of Oxford, Knewstub and Chaderton of Cambridge.

25. Reverend Harold Kirk-White, *William Brewster: The Father of New England* (Boston, Lincs.: Richard Kay, 1992), 77.

SCROOBY

1. The great church of Southwell, famous for its exquisite medieval carvings of plants, among the first to be copied from life rather than from pattern books, has been a cathedral only since 1884. Before that, along with the almost equally impressive churches of Ripon and Beverly, it was a possession of the see of York.

2. The basic source for this chapter, as for so much of the history of the Pilgrims, is William Bradford, *Of Plymouth Plantation 1620–1647*, ed. Samuel Eliot Morison (New York: Random House, 1952). Other sources for this chapter include Winnifred Cockshott, *The Pilgrim Fathers: Their Church and Colony* (New York: Putnam, 1909); Dexter and Dexter, *The England and Holland of the Pilgrims*; Francis Dillon, *A Place for Habitation*; Kirk-White, *William Brewster*.

3. Francis J. Bremer, *John Winthrop: America's Forgotten Founding Father* (New York: Oxford University Press, 2003), 47.

4. Bradford, *Plymouth Plantation*, 325.

5. Kirk-White, *Brewster*, 60, quoting an early-seventeenth-century manuscript on sixty local parishes by the vicar of nearby Sheffield.

6. Cockshott, *Pilgrim Fathers*, 51.

7. Simon Jenkins, *England's Thousand Best Houses* (London: Penguin, 2003), 435, calls it, rightly, a "textbook of medieval architecture."

8. Dillon, *Place for Habitation*, 83. Bancroft, then Bishop of London, preached a "Warning against Puritans" at St. Paul's Cross in 1588.

9. Historians have traditionally said that three hundred were expelled, but Francis Dillon (*Place for Habitation*, 23), quoting S. R. Babbage, says the number should be ninety, some of whom were reinstated.

10. Morison (ed.), Introduction, in Bradford, *Plymouth Plantation*, xxiii, quoting Cotton Mather, *Magnalia Christi*, Lib. II, 3, 1702.

11. Bradford, *Plymouth Plantation*, 12.

12. There is some disagreement over how many Pilgrims made this stage of the journey. Dillon suggested there could not have been more than twenty to thirty, while the Dexters, followed by Morison, suggest 125. Kirk-White thinks this is too high. So do I.

13. Bradford, *Plymouth Plantation*, 13.

The Waters of Exile

1. Simon Schama, *The Embarrassment of Riches: An Interpretation of Dutch Culture in the Golden Age* (New York: HarperCollins, 1987).

2. My account of the Pilgrims' sojourn in Leiden owes much to Joke Kardux and Eduard van der Bilt, *Newcomers in an Old City: The American Pilgrims in Leiden 1609–1620* (Leiden: Burgersdijk & Niermans, 1998). The classic account is H. M. Dexter and M. Dexter, *The England and Holland of the Pilgrims*.

3. Keith L. Sprunger, *Dutch Puritanism: A History of the English and Scottish Churches of the Netherlands in the Sixteenth and Seventeenth Centuries* (Leiden: Brill, 1982).

4. *Stincksteeg* was a generic term for any little back alley, not the name of this particular street.

5. The following description of Pilgrim worship is based on that in Kirk-White, *William Brewster*, 114, which is based on two works by John Smyth, *Advertisement* and *Plea for Infants*.

6. Arminius, born in 1560, died in 1609, the year the Pilgrims reached Holland.

7. Bradford, *Plymouth Plantation*, 25 n6.

8. Ibid., 28.

9. Dillon, *A Place for Habitation*, 84, 116.

10. Bradford, *Plymouth Plantation*, 37 n2.

11. Perry Miller, *Errand into the Wilderness* (Cambridge, MA: Belknap Press, 1956), 11.

12. See, for example, Theodore Dwight Bozeman, *To Live Ancient Lives:*

The Primitivist Dimension in Puritanism (Chapel Hill, NC: University of North Carolina Press, 1988).

VOYAGE AND LANDFALL

1. He did write later saying he hoped to join the Pilgrims, but it is not clear whether he realistically contemplated doing so.

2. Ezra 8:1.

3. Artaxerxes I, in Persian Artakhshatra and later known as Ardeshir, was king of Persia from 465 to 424 BC. He belonged to the Achaemenid dynasty and was the successor of Xerxes I, the king defeated by the Greeks at Marathon.

4. They did not call themselves that. The name was given to them by William Bradford (*Plymouth Plantation*, 47): "So they left that good and pleasant city which had been their resting place near twelve years; but they knew they were pilgrims, and . . . lift up their eyes to the heavens, their dearest country, and quieted their spirits."

5. Delfshaven (the Dutch spelling) is now absorbed into the great port of Rotterdam, the busiest port in Europe.

6. This meant the ship could carry sixty tons of merchandise or goods. Modern ships are rated by the deadweight of the vessel.

7. Jeremy Bangs, "Toward a Revision of the Pilgrims: Three New Pictures," *New England Historical and Genealogical Register* 153 (January 1999): 7–18, 21–2, 28. The painting is by Adam Willaerts, and is entitled "Departure of the Pilgrims from Delfshaven," 1620. It is reproduced in Kardux and van der Bilt, *Newcomers in an Old City*, p. 53.

8. Bradford, *Plymouth Plantation*, 47.

9. This is the conclusion of Joke Kardux and Eduard van der Bilt, *Newcomers in an Old City*, 74, who give the names of all but a few of the children. But estimates have varied. The Dexters, *England and Holland of the Pilgrims*, 650, says twenty-five. Researchers at Plimoth Plantation say "18 married couples (15 with children), six married men without their wives . . . eight servants." Plimoth Plantation with Peter Arenstam, John Kemp, and Catherine O'Neill Grace, *Mayflower 1620* (Washington, DC: National Geographic, 2003).

10. Kardux and van der Bilt, *Newcomers in an Old City*, 74–75.

11. It has been suggested, by Bargs, that "strangers," in the then accepted sense of foreigners, might have referred to Flemish or French-speaking

Protestants who accompanied the Pilgrims. There may have been some on board, but "strangers" seems to refer to the passengers who joined the Leiden contingent at Southampton.

12. Possibly the same name as "Coffin," later a well-established New England name.

13. Oxford English Dictionary, under "shallop" and "sloop." The difference between a shallop and a cutter is apparently that the former has a bowsprit and a jib.

14. Minions and sakers were relatively small guns, weighing between 9 and 13 hundredweight, or between a half and three-quarters of a ton. (H. R. Schubert, *History of the British Iron and Steel Industry* (London: Routledge & Kegan Paul, 1957).) Another authority, cited by Kirk-White (*William Brewster*), says a saker, or "sacre," weighed 1,500 pounds, and had a 3.5-inch bore and a range of 360 yards, while a minion weighed 1,200 pounds and had a 3.25-inch bore and a range of 340 yards.

15. They sold "three or four-score firkins," that is between 3,360 and 4,720 pounds of butter, according to S. E. Morison's calculations, or between one and a half and two tons.

16. The list is taken from Plimoth Plantation, *Mayflower 1620*, 19. Tuns, hogsheads, firkins, and terces are all different sizes of barrels.

17. James McDermott, *Martin Frobisher* (New Haven, CT: Yale University Press, 2001).

18. "This makes sense," comments Admiral Morison, an experienced yachtsman. "Any wooden vessel, if overmasted and given more sail than she can carry, will labor in a seaway, open her seams and spew her oakum." Bradford, *Plymouth Plantation*, 53 n3.

19. It has been suggested that this was the screw from the Leiden printing press.

20. Bradford, *Plymouth Plantation*, 58.

21. See Dava Sobel, *Longitude* (London: Penguin, 1996).

22. See, for example, Ernle Bradford, *Ulysses Found* (London: Hodder and Stoughton, 1963).

23. Martin de Hoyarsabal, *Voyages Avantureux* (Rouen: Du Petit Val, 1579).

24. Bradford, *Plymouth Plantation*, 60. See also Morison's footnote on that page.

25. The document known as *Mourt's Relation* is a collection of writings published in London in 1622. Its authorship is problematic. With an introduction signed G. Mourt, who may or may not have been one of the

Mayflower passengers called George Morton, some of the book may have been written by Robert Cushman, and some contributed by William Bradford, who also seems to have used the *Relation* in composing his own text, *Of Plymouth Plantation*. But most of *Mourt's Relation* was probably written by Edward Winslow, the Worcester printer who had helped William Brewster with the Leiden printing press. (See Dwight B. Heath (ed.) *Mourt's Relation: A Journal of the Pilgrims at Plymouth* (Bedford, MA: Applewood Books, 1963.) Winslow was something of a booster, minimizing the cold of the New England winter and failing altogether to mention either the constant threat of famine or the sickness that carried away half the Pilgrims in little more than two months.

A PLACE OF HABITATION

1. Bradford, *Plymouth Plantation*, 443–44.

2. Cotton Mather, *Magnalia Christi Americana*, vol. 1 (Hartford, CT: Silus Andras & Son, 1853), 111.

3. For example in Ernest Gebler's novel, *The Plymouth Adventure: A Chronicle Novel of the Voyage of the Mayflower* (New York: Doubleday, 1950), made into a Hollywood movie, *Plymouth Adventure* (1952), with Gene Tierney as Dorothy Bradford.

4. See George Ernest Bowman, "Governor William Bradford's First Wife Dorothy (May) Bradford Did Not Commit Suicide," *Mayflower Descendant* 29, 3 (July 1931), 97–102.

5. Heath (ed.), *Mourt's Relation*, 21.

6. Francis's brother, John Jr., later ran off and had to be brought back from a Nauset Indian village. In 1630 Francis's father, John Billington, was the first member of the Plymouth community hanged for "wilful murder." Six years later his wife was sentenced to sit in the stocks and to be whipped for slander.

7. The dictionary definition is "one of various kinds of blowing, spouting, blunt-headed, delphinoid cetaceans." There seem to be two animals that have been known as grampuses: Risso's dolphin (*grampus griseus*) and the killer whale (*Orcinus orca*) which hunts seals and even, on occasion, other whales. From *Mourt's* description, *Orcinus orca* seems more likely.

8. J. Keith Cheetham, *On the Trail of the Pilgrim Fathers* (Edinburgh: Luath Press, 2001). Morison says it is not clear that the Pilgrims landed on "the

large boulder since called Plymouth Rock." The rock was "first identified in 1741 by Elder John Faunce, aged 95, as 'the place where the forefathers landed,' and although he probably only meant to say that they used it as a landing place, for it would have been very convenient for that purpose at half tide, everyone seems to have assumed that 'they' first landed there. The exploring party may have landed anywhere between Captain's Hill and the Rock."

9. Heath (ed.), *Mourt's Relation*, 41.

10. Edward Winslow, *Good Newes From New England* (Bedford, MA: Applewood Books, [1624] 1996), 89 n9.

11. Bradford, *Plymouth Plantation*, 76.

12. Extracted by Patricia Scott Deetz and James Deetz, The Plymouth Colony Archive Project, Mayflower Passenger Deaths, 1620–21, from Thomas Prince's *A Chronological History of New-England, in the Form of Annals* (Boston, N.E.: 1736; Edinburgh private printing, 1887–1888), 5 vols. In volume 3, Prince lists at intervals extracts from "A Register of Governor Bradford's in his own hand, recording some of the first deaths, marriages and punishments at Plymouth."

FIRST ENCOUNTERS

1. I have followed Edward Winslow's account in *Mourt's Relation*, 50–59, which is much fuller than Bradford's and also more nearly contemporary, as Bradford's account was written not earlier than 1634.

2. J. Franklin Jameson, *Narratives of New Netherland, 1609–1664* (New York: Scribner, 1909), 112. De Rasières was a Dutchman of French Huguenot descent, described by Bradford as New Amsterdam's "chief merchant, and second to the Governor, a man of a fair and genteel behavior."

3. David S. Jones, *Rationalizing Epidemics: Meanings and Uses of American Indian Mortality since 1600* (Cambridge, MA: Harvard University Press, 2004), 24.

4. Daniel K. Richter, *Facing East from Indian Country: A Native History of Early America,* (Cambridge MA: Harvard University Press, 2001).

5. Karen Ordahl Kupperman, *Indians and English* (Ithaca, NY: Cornell University Press, 2000) 34, quoting John Brereton, *Briefe and true Relation of the Discoverie of the North Part of Virginia.*

6. Alden T. Vaughan, *New England Frontier, Puritans and Indians 1620–1625* (Norman, OK: University of Oklahoma Press, 1995), 27.

7. The Bering land bridge, caused by a lowering of ocean levels when water was locked up in the polar ice cap, appears to have been open to migration at several periods in the past, including 40,000–45,000 years ago, 33,000–28,000 years ago, and 23,000–13,000 years ago.

8. Vaughan, *New England Frontier*, 41–42.

9. Ibid., 58.

10. Ibid., 46–47.

11. Douglas E. Leach, *Flintlock and Tomahawk* (New York: Norton, 1958), 200.

12. Jones, *Rationalizing Epidemics*, 23.

13. From Samuel de Champlain, *Les Voyages du Sieur de Champlain Xainteongeois* (Paris, 1613), reproduced in Jones, *Rationalizing Epidemics*, 25, by permission of the Houghton Library, Harvard University.

14. Jones, *Rationalizing Epidemics*, 29.

15. Ibid., 26.

16. Richter, *Facing East*, 97.

17. Ibid., 59.

18. Ibid., 27, citing Gorges.

19. Kupperman, *Indians and English*, 78.

20. Ibid., 63, quoting George Percy, "Observations Gathered out of a Discourse of the Plantation of the Southerne Colonie in Virginia by the English, 1606."

21. Ibid., 75.

THE LOSS OF TRUST

1. Daniel Gookin was made superintendent of the Indians in Massachusetts, in which post he was said to have taken an "intelligent and humane" interest in them. He wrote two books on the Indians, *Historical Collections of the Indians in New England*, written in 1674 (published 1792), and *The Doings and Sufferings of the Christian Indians*, completed in 1677 (published 1836).

2. Leach, *Flintlock and Tomahawk*, 6.

3. Vaughan, *New England Frontier*, 89.

4. Bradford, *Plymouth Plantation*.

5. Ibid., 152.

6. Leach, *Flintlock and Tomahawk*, 242.

THE COLONY

1. Sir Ferdinando Gorges was born in Somerset, England, c. 1565. He founded the Plymouth and London companies for colonizing New England, and made many attempts to found colonies, especially in Maine. Gorges died in 1647.

2. By Morison, in Bradford, *Plymouth Plantation*, 37 n2.

3. Winslow, *Good Newes From New England*, 53.

4. Bradford, *Plymouth Plantation*, 121.

5. Cushman's sermon, "The Sin and Danger of Self Love," is published in full by Caleb Johnson on his Web site, http://members.aol.com/Calebj/sermon.html.

6. Bremer, *John Winthrop*, 238.

7. Durand Echevarria, *A History of Billingsgate* (Wellfleet, MA: Wellfleet Historical Society, 1991), 12.

8. Bradford, *Plymouth Plantation*, 253.

9. Magna Carta. Article 39. "No freemen shall be taken or imprisoned or disseised or exiled or in any way destroyed, nor will we go upon him nor send upon him, except by the lawful judgment of his peers or by the law of the land. Article 40. To no one will we sell, to no one will we refuse or delay, right or justice." See William Stubbs, *Select Charters and Other Illustrations of English Constitutional History from the Earliest Times to the Reign of Edward the First* (Holmes Beach, FL: Gaunt Inc., 1996). For Plymouth Code, see Web site, http://personal.pitnet.net/primarysources/plymouth.html.

10. Bradford, *Plymouth Plantation*, 334.

FASTS AND THANKSGIVINGS

1. The Breeches Bible was so called because in it, at Genesis 3:7, Adam and Eve "sewed themselves fig leaves and made themselves breeches," rather than aprons, as earlier and later translations put it. John Wyclif was the first translator of the Bible into English in the early fifteenth century. In 1525–26, William Tyndale produced a new translation direct from the original Hebrew and Greek, which was the first to be printed. In 1539, Henry VIII produced the first royal translation, largely the work of Miles Coverdale, known as the Great Bible. The Geneva Bible, or Breeches Bible, first published in 1560, was produced in Geneva by English Protestant refugees and was beloved of Protestants and Puritans.

2. Telephone interview with John B. Thomas, November 2005.

3. Exodus 23:16: "the feast of ingathering, at the end of the year, when thou gatherest in thy labors out of the field!"; Leviticus 23:39–44.

4. The following account owes much to William DeLoss Love, *The Fast and Thanksgiving Days of New England* (Boston, New York: Houghton and Mifflin, 1895).

5. Winslow, *Good Newes From New England*, 56.

6. Love, *Fast and Thanksgiving Days of New England*, passim.

A Republic Gives Thanks

1. Matthew Dennis, *Red, White, and Blue Letter Days: An American Calendar* (Ithaca, NY: Cornell University Press, 2002), 85.

2. By Matthew Dennis, *Red, White and Blue Letter Days*, 88.

3. This account of Sarah Hale draws heavily on Amy Condra Peters, "Godey's Lady's Book and Sarah Josepha Hale: Making Female Education Fashionable," *Loyola University Student Historical Journal* 24 (1992–93), 43–48.

4. So-called because before being elected governor he was a flour salesman and songwriter whose campaign song was written for the Light Crust Doughboys.

Epilogue: The Invention of a Tradition

1. Eric Hobsbawm and Terence Ranger (eds.), *The Invention of Tradition* (Cambridge, UK: Cambridge University Press, 1920).

Index

Index

Index

PUBLICAFFAIRS is a publishing house founded in 1997. It is a tribute to the standards, values, and flair of three persons who have served as mentors to countless reporters, writers, editors, and book people of all kinds, including me.

I. F. STONE, proprietor of *I. F. Stone's Weekly,* combined a commitment to the First Amendment with entrepreneurial zeal and reporting skill and became one of the great independent journalists in American history. At the age of eighty, Izzy published *The Trial of Socrates,* which was a national bestseller. He wrote the book after he taught himself ancient Greek.

BENJAMIN C. BRADLEE was for nearly thirty years the charismatic editorial leader of *The Washington Post.* It was Ben who gave the *Post* the range and courage to pursue such historic issues as Watergate. He supported his reporters with a tenacity that made them fearless, and it is no accident that so many became authors of influential, best-selling books.

ROBERT L. BERNSTEIN, the chief executive of Random House for more than a quarter century, guided one of the nation's premier publishing houses. Bob was personally responsible for many books of political dissent and argument that challenged tyranny around the globe. He is also the founder and was the longtime chair of Human Rights Watch, one of the most respected human rights organizations in the world.

. . .

For fifty years, the banner of Public Affairs Press was carried by its owner, Morris B. Schnapper, who published Gandhi, Nasser, Toynbee, Truman, and about 1,500 other authors. In 1983 Schnapper was described by *The Washington Post* as "a redoubtable gadfly." His legacy will endure in the books to come.

Peter Osnos, *Founder and Editor-at-Large*